The Great I Am and I

*My Journey into and from the Heart of God
in the Midst and Aftermath of Apartheid/Segregation in South Africa*

MARLENE FERREIRA

Unless otherwise indicated, all Scripture quotations are taken from the NEW AMERICAN STANDARD BIBLE®, Copyright ©1960,1962,1963,1968,1971,1972,1973,1975,1977,19 95 by The Lockman Foundation. Used by permission.

Scripture quotations marked (AMP) are taken from the Amplified® Bible, Copyright © 2015 by The Lockman Foundation Used by permission

Scripture quotations marked (NLT) are taken from the Holy Bible, New Living Translation, copyright © 1996, 2004, 2007 by Tyndale House Foundation. Used by permission of Tyndale House Publishers, Inc., Carol Stream, IL 60188. All rights reserved.

All emphasis within Scripture quotations is the author's own. Please note that the name satan and related names are not capitalized. I choose not to acknowledge him, even to the point of violating grammatical rules.

Print ISBN: 978-1-950685-69-1
Ebook ISBN: 978-1-950685-70-7

CONTENTS

Preface v

In Memory of Doris and Elwood Norris vii

Prologue xi

Introduction...xv

Chapter 1   Setting the Stage... 1

Chapter 2   The Joseph Mindset Requires Conviction.......19

Chapter 3   When A Calling Seems Paradoxical............... 31

Chapter 4   Midian A.k.a. The Silence of God 47

Chapter 5   God's Ways Are Not Our Ways.....................61

Chapter 6   "I Am Who I Am–The Lord" 83

Chapter 7   Home Is Where The Heart Is 105

Chapter 8   The Fear of God Versus The Fear of Man.....117

Chapter 9   The Exodus 131

Chapter 10   Emmanuel, God With Us............................ 146

Chapter 11   The Great I Am and His Uniting Power of Agape Love...163

About the Author...185

PREFACE

I grew up during the apartheid years in South Africa. *Apartheid* is the Afrikaans word for segregation. With the atrocities of apartheid fresh in my memory, I emerged from seminary to pastor my first congregation in the Dutch Reformed Church of South Africa. Apartheid had just been abolished. The African National Congress (ANC) had been voted in as the governing political party with Mr. Nelson Mandela at the helm, which ushered in a Black Majority Rule and was considered a great victory for Black people and for social justice in general. The oppressive White Minority Regime had been toppled. Unfortunately, on ground level, victory was short lived.

The ANC had made certain political promises to Black people, one of them being that if they voted for them, they would give White peoples' properties and possessions to the Blacks as soon as they were in office. Thousands of Black farm workers migrated to the outskirts of major cities waiting for the ANC to come into power, so that they could walk in and claim their homes and businesses from the White people. Others stayed where they were, hoping to claim as their own the farms where they were living and working. A type of theology was being promoted that equated the Black people who were oppressed during apartheid with the Israelite slaves who were oppressed by the Egyptians. The abolishment of apartheid was touted as their exodus into freedom, which included plundering the Whites, or the so-called Egyptians, like Israel of old did before heading for the Promised Land!

The ANC could not make good on their promise though, because legally the properties belonged to their owners; as a result, an angry killing spree began that still continues today. Whites and their families were murdered in droves. The Black people who moved to the outskirts of cities became squatters there, living in poverty under horrible conditions. Violence in the squatter camps escalated, and a multitude of Black people were murdered as well, and all of it still continues today. Bloodshed is almost as common as breathing in South Africa.

At the time of this writing, it has been twenty-five years since the ANC took over and apartheid was abolished; yet South Africa is still reeling under escalating racism, hatred, poverty and violence. To make matters worse, the country's infrastructure is falling into disarray because of a lack of maintenance and mismanagement of government and municipal funds on all fronts, as well as a self-seeking lust for power, fame and fortune by many of her leaders.

When I entered the ministry, emotions were raw on all sides. The confrontation that followed left most of those involved, including me, wounded and broken. I eventually resigned the Dutch Reformed Church, licking my wounds and reeling in grief. As I tried to make sense out of it all, I turned to God for answers. After tripping over my own wounds and scars and grief for years, God finally brought me to a place of restoration and understanding through the life of Moses. He led me on a journey through the pages of Exodus and, through Moses' life, giving me understanding of my own life and calling. He finally revealed to me His heart for mankind and showed me why humanity finds it so hard to love. He taught me that racial discrimination is spiritual at its root, and that we'll never solve the issue if we don't address the root.

It is my prayer that as you read this book, you will encounter the Author of true love, as depicted by me through my life and the life of Moses, and that you will be challenged to go forth from the heart of God and create a world where racism and racial discrimination is abolished by a love that only He can deliver.

In Memory of Doris
and Elwood Norris

Elwood *loved* the Lord, but he would tell you, "Mama *knew* the Lord."

Doris introduced me to levels of intimacy in the Lord that I thought only Biblical characters could have.

After Doris's death, the Lord showed me a picture of Doris holding a specific ember of His anointing. Her assignment was to kindle that ember and keep it burning until it was deposited into a very specific recipient. Doris actually kindled many embers, which she deposited into many people; but this one was for me. God allowed me to see just how faithfully Doris kept that ember alive, even sometimes at a great cost, and how she carefully and lovingly deposited it into me over time.

For some reason, Doris got to nurture the seed, and I get to be ablaze with the germination of it. Whenever I get to minister in His name, I will be ablaze for the both of us, ministering a part of His anointing to others that she so faithfully nurtured. Doris passed on many things to each of her family and friends, but what a humbling thought that God also sent a young South African woman to America to meet a great grandmother who was called to nurture and pass an ember of spiritual anointing to her.

Elwood lived from May 9, 1922, to January 2, 2012. Doris lived from August 8, 1923, till the end of March 2016. I met them in 2002, and I thank God for fourteen rich years of friendship. This book was quite a journey, the initial stages taken over the course of two years while tending to Doris in her final years of heart and kidney failure. I can't thank her enough for her encouragement and belief in me.

Looking back, several others also deposited their share of His heart in me, preparing the soil of my heart for true relationship with Him. This book brings tribute to all the spiritual mentors in my life—past, present and future.

Ann Hiemstra, my longtime friend and mentor from South Africa, is actually the catalyst for my writing this book. She insisted I write my story and painstakingly went through every chapter to help with grammar and flow and challenged me every step of the way. Thank you so much for your patience and honest review.

I would also like to thank Lorraine and Doug Roberts and Paul Norris for reading and critiquing and giving me feedback, Jane and Owusu Asamoah and Maureen Anderson for their generous contributions in the editing and publication process, Angie and Beth for their professional services in the final editing and publication of this book.

Lastly, there is Jim and Nita Tarter who came alongside me after Doris's death, while I was still completing this book. Thank you for helping me process very difficult months.

Holy Spirit worked in miraculous ways through people to get this book written and published and I am deeply indebted to Him and the people who listened to His voice.

Thank You Holy Spirit, for inspiring me to write and others to encourage and support me. Thank you for showing us Your heart. I love You so much!

PROLOGUE

SIX YEARS OLD AND SEEKING . . .

I was six years old when I first became aware of spirituality and of Something or Someone calling me deeper.

My dad was a fitter and turner, and therefore in high demand with the gold mines, doing what was known as shaft sinking. The mine companies were digging shafts and tunnels with high technology machinery, which my dad helped maintain and build, as they established gold mines. This meant that we never stayed in one place for very long. Once the mine shaft had been dug and established, my dad had to move on to the next job.

When my parents finally decided to end their nomadic lifestyle and settle down, they chose Virginia, a small town in the Free State in South Africa. My paternal grandmother lived there, and it was a booming gold mining community. They were looking for more stability and wanted to settle into community life and be closer to my grandmother. My dad was able to secure a permanent job at the mine and work towards becoming a mechanical engineer, and my mom planned to establish herself as an employee in a bank. I had just started first grade, and their move meant a stable school life for me.

At the time, my parents did not attend church, but my grandmother did. I loved to stay with my grandmother on weekends, which meant I got to go to church with her on Sundays; at least, that's how I viewed it at the time. Many years later, she told me I was the one who had taken her to church. That is not how I remember it, though I do remember walking to church by myself, just up the street from her apartment, when she didn't feel like going.

I remember registering myself for Sunday school, which was like a genuine school that you attended after church on Sundays with tests and exams. At the end of the year, we wrote a big exam and had to pass in order to progress to the following year—at least, that's what we were told. The inference was, you couldn't become a member of the church as an adult if you hadn't passed these exams, though there were always exceptions.

I couldn't stay away from church, regardless of whether my grandmother accompanied me. The minister, Rev. Oliphant, was a compelling speaker. I hung on his every word. I never went to children's church because I just couldn't miss his sermons. They were not only compelling, but also inspiring, uplifting. More so, they made me feel closer to that Someone or Something tugging at my spirit. I hardly ever missed a Sunday and fought my parents hammer and tongs if they didn't want me to visit Grandma for a weekend. I *had to go!* My parents didn't understand, and I couldn't explain because I really didn't understand either.

I loved my grandmother—she passed away a few years ago—and I wanted to be with her as much as possible; but I also saw her as a gateway to Rev. Oliphant and that Something or Someone mystical. Rev. Oliphant and his sermons became a point of contact, connecting me to my mystical calling that was becoming stronger by the day.

Then there was Mrs. Bester, my first- to third-grade teacher. She taught all three grades at the same time in the same room. I loved it because when I had done my first-grade work, I could just carry on with the work the other grades were doing.

Mrs. Bester was a gifted storyteller who could make the stories of the Bible come alive! Everybody loved story time. We would gather on the carpet as a group, and she would start a Bible story. Pretty soon, you could literally hear a pin drop in the classroom, not because she was the teacher and we were compelled to listen, but because she took you to church. You could feel, taste, and hear the Bible characters and events. She engaged all our senses and took us on wonderful Bible adventures.

Rev. Oliphant and Mrs. Bester fueled an insatiable hunger for the Bible in me but, more importantly, for the God of the Bible. Was He still working in people's lives the way He did in the Biblical characters' lives? Could I have the same relationship with Him as they did? Could I possibly become a Moses or a Joshua or a Solomon or one of the others while I was on this earth? These questions didn't all arise at the same time; they gradually developed over years. As I grew up, they became louder and more numerous.

Several years ago, while taking care of Doris, I started writing the contents of this book for myself during my quiet times with the Lord. I wanted to understand the character of Moses better and investigate the relationship between God and Moses and Israel; ultimately, I was trying to determine how I could get in on that action. How could I be a Moses and a Solomon to my generation? How could I be like Jesus and whatever God's highest is for me and through me in Christ? I aim to share these revelations with you so that you too can discover His highest for you and through you.

As you read, it is my prayer that through the story of Moses and Israel and my own testimony in this book, you will enter into heavenly realms in Christ (Ephesians 2:6) and that we can experience together the God of the Covenant, entering history in real time, intervening and becoming tangibly involved—changing peoples' and communities' and nations' lives forever.

I invite you to join me on a journey from an Egypt mindset (held hostage by a slavery and orphan spirit) into a kingdom mindset (set free in Christ) and beyond (there is more) as far as I have traveled thus far . . .

There is a Divine greatness developing in me, waiting to be born; and there is a tangible threat trying to destroy me and that Divine greatness. I am tangibly aware of this tug-of-war dynamic on a regular basis.

INTRODUCTION

Fruitfulness, Multiplication and Increase

"Be fruitful and multiply, and fill the earth, and subdue it." – Genesis 1:28

My grandmother used to tell me on a regular basis, "God only helps those who help themselves." She wanted me to have a disciplined work ethic, because she wanted me to succeed.

I understand her intent, and I deeply appreciate the work ethic she and my parents instilled in me, but the statement she made was not Biblical. Instead of it coming out of the pages of the Bible, it came from a place of hardship and offence at God. Her other regular saying was, "God has His favorites, and I'm not one of them."

As a young child, she and her siblings were products of the Great

Depression. She learned to fight for survival as an orphan growing up in poverty, being passed on from family to family, working long, hard hours on family farms, walking to school with bare feet, yearning to belong.

Love and abundance was not something she knew. As an adult, she and her husband endured the Second World War with him fighting in Europe. After the war, she lost her husband at a young age to lung cancer and was forced to fend for herself and become very independent. She invested in friends and causes with fervor, but ultimately, she never did know the true love of God and His ways even though she believed in Him as her Lord and Savior. She multiplied financially based on her own abilities, which were quite extraordinary, but in the end, she helplessly watched it all crumble due to no fault of her own.

My grandmother eventually died alone, sick and stripped of everything for which she had worked so hard. But an even sadder and more important reality is, she never could relinquish her orphan spirit for the true Spirit of God and, as a result, she never could embrace His highest *for* her and *through* her, which goes far beyond ability and achievements.

Even though she once achieved great heights financially and socially, the orphan in her prevailed; and society and loved ones, even me, took advantage of that. We often used her for what she was able to give and very seldom just loved her for who she was. She gave generously, the orphan in her hoping to buy love in return; but the return was often lacking. I write this in great tenderness and admiration and gratitude for who she was and the role she played in my life and others' lives. She was a very special individual, which is why her death was so upsetting to me and really made me become introspective.

Fruitfulness, multiplication, increase and authority outside of a personal relationship with God in Christ, or even a God-centered life like my grandmother but plagued by an orphan spirit, becomes a self-centered limited force that is always eventually physically, mentally and ultimately spiritually destructive. Inside of Jesus, though, it brings life and hope and miraculous abundance and growth far beyond self, leaving a supernaturally blessed heritage for generations to come. My grandmother left me a heritage of wonderful memories, but also a very strong reminder that life is fleeting, and if we're not investing in eternity, it is all for naught.

Just to be sure that there is no confusion, when I refer to God, I'm *not* referring to Buddha, or Allah, or the Universal god, or any other. I am specifically referring to Yahweh, the God of Abraham, Isaac, Jacob and Jesus, the God of the Covenant, the Great I AM—Father, Son and Holy Spirit. He is the God of true love relationships.

Increase is hardwired into our DNA.

A mathematician by the name of Leonardo Pisano, nicknamed Fibonacci, who lived in the 1100s and 1200s, proved that rabbits multiplied according to a special number sequence which was later called the Fibonacci sequence. Since then, scientists and mathematicians have concluded that all living things—humans, plants, animals, cells, storm systems, markets which by design are driven by human emotion—grow and diminish according to these number sequences.

Who knew? There is an order, a Divine order, hardwired into this creation and into people that promotes and requires growth. Not only does God command people to increase in Genesis, but there is actually scientific and mathematical proof that growth and increase have been hardwired into our DNA

Unfortunately, man sinned and was separated from God according to Genesis 3:24, causing this hardwired trait of growth and multiplication to become a curse. Multiplication without a personal relationship with the Creator and His blessing and favor results in over-utilized, impoverished land, poverty, social degradation, oppression, dictatorship, sickness and disease—in short, the abominable results of sin.

Some nations have established extreme measures to control and limit multiplication, hence law-enforced birth control, abortions, murder, restrictions on land ownership, etc. Their problem, however, is not multiplication; their problem is separation from and disregard for God. Outside of a personal relationship with the living Covenant God, man runs out of room, which results in a self-centered fight for space and survival.

Blessing and curse—two sides of the same coin called multiplication

"Be fruitful and multiply, and fill the earth, and subdue it." – Genesis 1:28

When man is in relationship with the Covenant God, multiplication is a blessing, and God will actually expand the environment and resources as part of His blessing to accommodate growth. Read Deuteronomy 28:1-14. When this God and His covenantal favor is rejected, multiplication becomes a nightmare, causing people groups to fiercely compete for survival as limited resources and space dwindle and sickness and disease spread rampantly. Read Deuteronomy 28:15-68.

Below is a simplified comparison between the blessing and the curse as depicted in Deuteronomy 28:1-68 as pertaining to nations. How a nation responds to God on a corporate level not only determines God's favor or judgment on that nation, but also has profound effects on its people as individuals and communities. Every nation as a corporate entity is given ample opportunity by God to choose either the blessing or the curse.

BLESSING (Deuteronomy 28:1-14)	CURSE (Deuteronomy 28:15-68)
Nations who obey and serve the Lord, faithfully honoring His Name, also on governmental and community levels. Below are the blessings they receive.	Nations who disobey His Word and refuse to fear and honor His Name, also on governmental and community level. Below is the curse that befalls them.
International recognition, leadership, mentorship and blessings that surpass natural limitations (28:1, 2)	An abomination in the sight of the world; total destruction (hunger, thirst, nakedness, lack, capture and terrible oppression, total despair) (28:48, 65-67)
Cities and farms will prosper. (28:3)	Cities and farms will go bankrupt and decay. (28:16)
Many healthy, thriving newborns (28:4)	Newborns will be cursed. (many hardships) (28:18)

Many healthy, thriving animal offspring (28:4)	Livestock offspring will be cursed. (many hardships) (28:18)
Herds (income) will increase continuously. (28:4)	Income will decrease continuously. (28:18)
Abundance of groceries and food supplies (28:5)	Groceries dwindle – becomes harder and harder to put food on the table (28:17)
Safe and secure personal and public life (28:6)	No safety and security anywhere (28:19)
Any attacks against the nation will be thwarted by the Lord Himself. (28:7)	The Lord Himself will send curses, confusion and rebuke until the nation is destroyed. (28:20)
Savings, earnings, jobs, country and economy will prosper. (28:8)	Nothing that people put their hands to will prosper. (28:20)
Established as God's own special holy nation – the apple of God's eye (28:9)	Cursed by God, out of His favor (28:20, 21)
Other nations will recognize God in such a nation and be afraid of its people, respecting them as a nation under God's protection. (28:10)	People will rise up against such a nation and destroy and terrorize its people. (28:25)
Prosperity will abound and affect every aspect of life on a personal and national level. (28:11)	Such a nation will be denied access to the prosperity of the earth and the sky – all attempts to tap into earthly and heavenly provision will be thwarted by hardships. (28:23)
Such a nation will have supernatural provisions rain down on its people all the time. (28:12)	God's supernatural calamity will rain down on such a nation continuously as judgment. (28:24)
This nation will never have to borrow and will have a surplus to lend to other nations. (28:12)	The foreigners in this nation will prosper, and its own people will become debtors to the foreigners. (28:44)
This nation will be at the cutting edge of everything – leading the way internationally. (28:13)	The foreigners in this nation will excel and be on the cutting edge while its own will gradually lose all esteem and influence. (28:43)
	Horrible diseases for which there is no cure will overtake its people. (28:21, 22, 26, 27-29, 35, 59-62)
	Death will be so rampant that there will be nobody to bury the dead and bodies will be eaten by wild animals and birds. (28:26)

	Everything dear to the people, including their family, will be taken away from them, and the people themselves will be oppressed and crushed continuously. (28:30-33)
	Constant calamity will cause mental depravity. (28:34)
	In spite of hard labor, people will never reap a harvest because of pestilence and insects wreaking havoc with crops. This nation and its people will be financially ruined. (28:38-40, 42)
	Eventually the entire nation will be invaded and its people (adults and children) kidnapped and taken to foreign countries where they will be forced to worship other gods and taunted all day long. (28:36-37, 49-52, 63-68)
	Those who remain after the invasion will be so hungry that they will resort to cannibalism. (28:53-58)

The truth is, without God's merciful regular intervention, the entire human race would eventually cease to exist on this earth, because, for selfish reasons, the majority of nations and individuals always seem to choose the curse. You only have to watch ten minutes of the news to know that evil, which often translates into natural disasters, sicknesses and diseases, terrorism, racial wars and other wars, poverty and moral depravity, is growing at an horrendous pace. Deuteronomy 28:15-68 would suggest that it is because nations as corporate entities are generally choosing the curse, and the Bible is clear that every nation will eventually have its day of reckoning with God in this lifetime. Nations get judged now, individuals get judged with the Second Coming of Jesus. Genesis 15:13-16 and Matthew 23:32-36 are good references to the principle that nations will be judged in this lifetime.

The Scriptural inference is that by corporately making the right choice as a nation, our nation, your nation can be recipients of the blessing, but where does it start? How do we get a nation to choose the blessing?

This is one of the questions I was asking God whilst watching South Africa plummet into poverty, violence and worse racial discrimination than ever before. Apartheid in itself brought an horrendous oppression to people groups, and the abolishment of apartheid exposed the damage of years of oppression; but instead of bringing healing, it produced new horrendous suffering and destruction and death. The curse was not broken; instead, it seemed to intensify. Why? The short answer is, even though apartheid was abolished on official governmental levels, it still lived on in the hearts of people in the form of racism, hatred, unforgiveness, fear, poverty, and the list goes on. Governmental laws cannot change the human heart, it can only manage it. So, how do we heal the heart and in turn, heal the land, the nation?

The bride of Christ, called the church, needs a heart adjustment.

"If my people who are called by My name, humble themselves and pray and seek my face and turn from their wicked ways, then I will hear from heaven and will forgive their sin and heal their land." – 2 Chronicles 7:14

The healing of a nation starts with repentance by the people called Christians, the people who profess Jesus Christ as their Lord and Savior irrespective of race or socio-economic background. Church, we must change our ways and our thinking. This is not a time for arrogance and pride and self-righteousness and judgment and pointing fingers and tossing nasty, hateful opinions—at least, not for the church. This is a time for humility and prayer and fasting and repentance. This is a time for all of God's children to go low on our hands and knees seeking the face of God, embracing Jesus and His forgiveness and redemption that came via the cross, confessing our waywardness and demonstrating the redemptive nature of Jesus in and through our lives.

Right now the world, not just South Africa, is in crisis; and it is in the midst of crises that humanity's weaknesses and sins are exposed.

After Adam and Eve sinned, they hid themselves from God because they realized for the first time, they were naked. It is in times of crises that we realize just how vulnerable our best attempts and successes really are; and suddenly we find ourselves at the mercy of God, and the fear of God grips us because we don't measure up. That's where the saying, "Oh, my God" comes from. Even unbelievers use it because they intuitively know they don't measure up.

The fear of God is actually a good thing. Proverbs tells us the fear of God is the beginning of wisdom. Proverbs also tells us that when we fear the Lord and turn away from evil, it will be healing to our bodies and refreshment to our bones.

Joshua understood this when he declared, *"As for me and my house, we will serve the Lord"* (Joshua 24:15). Joshua was a church prototype whose God centered leadership influenced an entire generation to serve God. Joshua 24:31 relates that *"Israel as a nation served the Lord all the days of Joshua and all the days of the elders who survived Joshua."* As a result, for a season, an entire nation, Israel, experienced supernatural prosperity.

The onus is not on the government to reform hearts; the onus is on the bride of Christ, God's children, the church. The onus is on *you*, dear child of God. Government maintains law and order, but God transforms hearts; and His children are His instruments for transformation, provided they themselves have been transformed!

Paul, who underwent radical personal transformation in Christ, understood the role of the church clearly when he wrote: *"For to me, to live is Christ and to die is gain"* (Philippians 1:21). If I may paraphrase Paul, he is saying, "As long as I'm alive, my entire life will revolve around Christ and bringing my influence circle into sync with His heart, even if it costs me my life. And when I die, I'll reap the reward of being 100% one with Him, my Lord and Savior, leaving behind a legacy of His presence and transformational power."

The last part of Hebrews 11 tells us of many believers who had the same mindset as Paul. Some of them, according to verses 33-38, *"by faith conquered kingdoms, performed acts of righteousness, obtained promises, shut the mouths of lions, quenched the power of fire, escaped the edge of the sword, from weakness were made strong, became mighty in war, put foreign armies to flight, received their children back from the dead by resurrection; others were tortured, experienced mocking and scourging, chains and imprisonment. Some were stoned, sawn in two, they were tempted, put to death, destitute, afflicted, ill-treated wandering in deserts and mountains and caves and holes in the ground."*

All of them had one thing in common—their faith in God; and together they built a people movement which stands on the foundation called Christ. Then for generation after generation, they handed the baton to the next generation and the next and the next, growing that movement up into a generation of believers who, according to John 15:7, will eventually become so united in Christ that they can ask whatever they want, and it be given to them because their desire is His desire, and His desire is their desire.

Paul tells us in 1 Corinthians 3:12, *"If anyone builds on this foundation"* . . . if anyone builds on the foundation called Christ using gold, silver, costly stones, wood, hay or straw, their work will be shown for what it is . . . because fire will come and test the quality of each person's work. Verse 14 states very clearly, *"If what has been built survives, the builder will receive a reward, if it's burned up, the builder will suffer loss but yet will be saved—even though only as one escaping through the flames."*

Dear child of God, what type of legacy are you leaving your children and your children's children and their children? First of all, is it really built on the foundation called Christ? Secondly, will it withstand the fires that spontaneously and unpredictably erupt around us? When the shaking comes, and it will, will it endure? Does the legacy that you are building, have Christ-like quality and durability and longevity? Can it cause an entire people group and even a nation to consider God and ultimately embrace Him?

Jesus left an astonishing promise behind in 1 John 15:7: *"If you remain in Me and My words remain in you, ask whatever you wish, and it will be done for you."* Solomon led a nation into that promise for a season, but he messed it up. Joshua led a nation into that promise with a glitch here and there, but the next generation messed it up. The disciples led a generation of church into that promise with a glitch here and there, but the next generation and the next and the next messed it up. Moses as an individual walked in that promise on a personal level for a season, and then messed up. Jesus walked it out as a man, fully man, while on this earth, and He did *not* mess it up.

He fulfilled His assignment on this earth, leaving an inheritance of resurrection life through His Spirit for His followers, provided they remained in Him and His words in them. Jesus made it possible for nations and individuals to *not* mess it up. What a legacy! And He modeled how we can tap into His legacy.

Jesus modeled what it looked like to be fully surrendered to God and therefore inherit the blessing. While He walked this earth, He modeled that He only did what He saw the Father do; and He only said what He saw the Father say through His relationship with Holy Spirit. He demonstrated how to pick up our cross and follow Him (Jesus) through Holy Spirit, in the context of a personal relationship with Father God, and therefore actually get to inherit and occupy and maintain the promise of not messing it up.

Paul encourages us in Hebrews 12:3 to *"consider Jesus . . . so that you will not grow weary and lose heart."* Job makes a profound statement in Job 42:5, *"I have heard of You by the hearing of the ear; But now my eye sees You; Therefore I retract, and I repent, sitting on dust and ashes."* When you actually meet, actually have a real encounter with the real Jesus, who is God, His presence has a way of reducing arrogance and pride and self-righteousness to dust and ashes. In His presence, all that remains is faith, hope and love, the greatest of which is love, according to Paul in 1 Corinthians 13:13.

The writer of Proverbs 3:6 states, *"In all your ways acknowledge Him and He will make your paths straight."* But acknowledging Him requires faith, and that's why Paul states in Hebrews 11:6, *"He who comes to God must believe that He is and that He is a rewarder of those who seek Him."*

As the church, we have to believe that Jesus is God's reward called redemption and restoration and reformation, which leads to transformation and we have to believe that Jesus is sufficient. Jesus paid the price on the cross for individual, generational, racial, ethnic, national, all sins; and in Him we are set free from them. We are grafted into Him as one united body, irrespective of race or gender, demonstrating His love, redemption and wisdom, bringing Godly solutions to crisis situations on individual, racial, ethnic, national and international levels and every and any other level. Jesus is sufficient, and in Him lies the only *real,* lasting solution for the broken state of the heart!

CHURCH!

"Arise, shine; for your light has come. And the glory of the Lord has risen upon you. For behold, darkness will cover the earth and deep darkness the peoples; but the Lord will rise upon you and His glory will appear upon you. Nations will come to your light, and kings to the brightness of your rising." – Isaiah 60:1-3

CHAPTER 1

Setting the Stage

"I am God Almighty, walk before me and be blameless. And I will make my Covenant between Me and you [Abram]), and will multiply you exceedingly." – Genesis 17:1-2

"I am God, the God of your father; do not be afraid to go down to Egypt, for I will make you [Jacob] a great nation there." – Genesis 46:3

God made a covenant with Abram in Genesis 17:2 to multiply him and his descendants exceedingly and eventually changed his name to Abraham. Jacob was a direct descendant of Abraham and a recipient of God's covenant, according to Genesis 46:3. Jacob obeys God and moves to Egypt at the invitation of his long-lost son, Joseph, with the Pharaoh's blessing. Jacob and his little family settle in Goshen in Egypt, then fast forward generations later: *"And the persons who came from the loins of Jacob were seventy in number, but Joseph was already in Egypt. Joseph died, and all his brothers and all that generation. But the sons of Israel [Jacob] were fruitful and increased greatly, and multiplied and became exceedingly mighty, so that the land was filled with them*" (Exodus 1:6-7).

After Joseph established his father's family in Egypt with help from the Pharaoh of that time, this little family grew. After the death of Joseph and the family members who first settled there, they had grown into a great nation of people filling the entire land of Egypt. That is some multiplication!

This is what the Covenant meant to Israel (Jacob): COVENANT initiated by the living God handed down from Abraham + obedience + relationship with the living God = multiplication, great nation, fruitfulness, increase, exceedingly mighty, land eventually filled with them = the blessing.

God is still the same yesterday, today and tomorrow. He is still the God of the Covenant. If we show our allegiance to Him by serving Him with our thoughts, words, deeds and bodies, He is faithful. Actually, sometimes He's faithful even in spite of our unfaithfulness. He promises in Hebrews 13:5, *"I will never desert you, nor will I ever forsake you."*

Decree with me, "My God is the God of the Covenant. He is faithful. He will never leave nor forsake me. Only in and through Him, will I be fruitful, multiply, fill and subdue the earth." And just to be clear, this process happens on His terms, not ours—a lesson that is often hard to learn but very rewarding once understood and embraced by the recipient.

A new Pharaoh with a new political ideology enters the scene.

"Now a new king arose over Egypt, who did not know Joseph." – Exodus 1:8

The Pharaohs of Egypt were not elected democratically by the people. They were born and honed into the role of king. All Pharaohs were believed to be representatives of the main Egyptian god, Ra; but in the minds of the Egyptian people, they were the manifestation of all the gods of Egypt in one, acting as authoritative mediators between the people and the gods. They supposedly achieved eternal life after death by becoming stars up in the heavens.

According to Wikipedia, a significant part of their role was to implement civil and religious rights, protect the vulnerable and weak, represent the country in foreign affairs, and be the Leader of the army—often fighting in person with the Egyptian troops. After a Pharaoh's death, a cult would often form around him. People would actually worship him; however, these cults were often short-lived.

Because the Pharaohs had direct contact with the gods, some were often left to reign as they pleased. After all, public opinion was that their decisions were being led by the gods and, therefore, whenever a new Pharaoh came into office, even though the Egyptian public did not know what to expect, they had full confidence that it would be good, because ultimately the gods were in charge through the Pharaoh.

This particular Pharaoh had just come into power. He was new, and so I imagine the political and social arenas were loaded with excitement and nervous anticipation. Several questions must have been lurking in people's minds. What power and paradigm shifts were going to take place? Whose comfort zones were going to be challenged? What kind of hardships and/or challenges would this change bring and to whom? Who would benefit and who would suffer?

Change was on the horizon for Egypt, and change is often a difficult pill to swallow, even when change is good, because ordinary folks get set in their ways. What kind of changes was this Pharaoh going to implement, and how would it affect the ordinary folks on the street?

This new king did not know Joseph.

It is worth noting about this new Pharaoh that he did not know Joseph. Who was Joseph again? Ah, yes. Joseph was that Israelite slave who worked for Potiphar and worshipped the God of the Covenant—the God of Abraham, Isaac and Jacob. Joseph was the man Potiphar sentenced to jail for a crime he didn't commit; in fact, Joseph spent several years of his life imprisoned as a result.

Joseph was also the man who was ultimately able to identify and interpret a dream that the previous Pharaoh had about a terrible drought that was coming to the world. Not only did this Joseph identify and interpret the dream correctly, but he was also able to lay out a course of action for the Pharaoh that would prevent Egypt from being a casualty of the looming drought. The Pharaoh was so impressed that he pardoned Joseph of his jail sentence and made him Prime Minister of Egypt, with the assignment to implement drought control measures.

Because of Joseph and his relationship with his Covenant God, Egypt and the rest of the world were able to sustain life through a drought. Egypt actually thrived under the leadership of Joseph because, while Egypt submitted to Joseph as their Prime Minister, God's favor on Joseph fell on Egypt. Egypt was directly blessed because of its relationship with Joseph and the God of the Covenant, and as long as Egypt kept treating Joseph's descendants well, the God of the Covenant kept blessing it as a world power. The Covenant was working in Egypt's favor.

This new Pharaoh had no idea that the reason he was enjoying prosperity was because of his connection with the descendants of Joseph and their God and the Covenant. This Pharaoh connected the current prosperity with the gods of Egypt and the fact that he himself represented those gods. True to tradition, he probably thought he was almost a deity himself, sovereign in his own eyes. As far as he was concerned, *he was it!* Mmmm, big mistake!

Pharaoh did not know Joseph, and he did not understand the Covenant. All he saw when he looked at the Israelites was that *"the people of the sons of Israel are more and mightier than we"* (Exodus 1:9).

Pharaoh's paranoia leads to Israel's bondage.

"Come, let us deal wisely with them, or else they will multiply and in the event of war, they will also join themselves to those who hate us, and fight against us and depart from the land." – Exodus 1:10

The Israelites were apparently no longer just in Goshen where the small family of Joseph originally settled. They had spread throughout the entire land of Egypt, according to Exodus 1:6-7. Pharaoh was considered the most powerful man in the world, and Egypt was the most powerful country. So, you can imagine his growing concern when he realized that the Israelites were outnumbering the Egyptians and becoming a powerful and mighty force as a people group in themselves. It was also a slap in the face to his pride, because the Israelites were herdsmen, and Egyptians despised herdsmen. Herdsmen were considered the lowest of the low, and here they were, surpassing the great and majestic Egyptian dynasty, the so-called best of the best.

Pharaoh started thinking about the possible repercussions it could have for Egypt, should Israel multiply even more, so he devised a plan: *"Come, let us deal wisely with them, or else they will multiply and in the event of war, they will also join themselves to those who hate us, and fight against us and depart from the land"* (Exodus 1:10).

Pharaoh had a two-fold plan that he felt sure would stunt their multiplication as well as their power and might. First of all, oppress and subdue them by enslaving them as a nation. According to him, this would break their power and might. *"So they appointed taskmasters over them to afflict them with hard labor"* (Exodus 1:11). Secondly, he set up a plan to kill all their baby boys. Pharaoh was certain this would stunt their multiplication and make their numbers come down.

So he commissioned the Israelite midwives, Shiphrah and Puah, to kill all the baby boys at birth. *"When you are helping the Hebrew women to give birth and see them upon the birth stool, if it is a son, then you shall put him to death; but if it is a daughter, then she shall live"* (Exodus 1:16).

However, we read in verse 17 that the midwives feared God and did not do as the Pharaoh said. Did I mention that the fear of God is the beginning of wisdom according to the Bible? So then the Pharaoh commanded all of Egypt to become involved themselves and spy on their pregnant Israelite neighbors. He commanded them as follows, *"Every son who is born, you are to cast into the Nile and every daughter you are to keep alive"* (Exodus 1:22).

When humans feel threatened, their primal instinct is to restrain, conquer and even kill in an attempt to protect themselves. When faced with a "true" threat, this instinct is validated; but often times till this very day, this instinct is used to demonstrate and enforce personal power and supremacy on levels for which it was never intended.

It's this very primal instinct that separates the Pharaohs from the Josephs. This Pharaoh's mindset was as follows: exalt yourself by manipulating and oppressing and enslaving others (Exodus 1:10-22). Joseph's mindset was very different: humble yourself before the God of the Covenant and the God of the Covenant will in due course perfect, confirm, strengthen and establish and exalt you (1 Peter 5:10; Genesis 39:1-6; Genesis 39:21-23; Genesis 41:39-41).

Pharaoh's tool for self-preservation, self-exaltation and supremacy was to oppress and kill.

"So they appointed taskmasters over them to afflict them with hard labor." – Exodus 1:11

"Every son who is born you are to cast into the Nile and every daughter you are to keep alive." – Exodus 1:22

The history of our world is full of stories about nations oppressing and murdering other nations all in the name of self-preservation and self-exaltation and supremacy. Hitler's Germany is probably one of the greatest examples in modern history of one nation oppressing and murdering another for the sake of self-exaltation and supremacy. Then there are the Tutsis killing the

Hutus for the same reason in Rwanda, Africa. What about early Europeans settling in America for the first time and the clash it caused with the indigenous native people of America? The list goes on for as far back as time has existed.

My memories are of South Africa where I grew up during the apartheid or segregation years. South Africa's history, leading up to apartheid, is full of tribal wars going way back to before the White settlers started arriving on her shores. Back then, the Xhosas and the Zulus were constantly fighting each other for power and supremacy over the land; then when the White settlers arrived, these two Black tribes turned their attention to the White people.

Eventually the controversy came to a head at the Battle of the Blood River. On the banks of this river, the White Boers, who would later become the Afrikaner Nation, and the Black Zulu nation confronted each other on opposite sides of the river—two different nationalities with two different belief systems. At this point in history, the Zulu nation was the strongest of the African tribes, and they worshipped their forefather spirits and other gods, while the Whites worshipped the God of the Covenant. Both groups held corporate prayer vigils before they faced each other on the banks of the Blood River.

The Whites were outnumbered exponentially that day. They knew they could potentially be wiped out. Actually, based on the numbers, it was a given that they could not survive. They needed a supernatural miracle. In their prayers, they asked the God of the Covenant to fight for them; and they promised that should He deliver them from the Zulus, they would commemorate that day throughout generations to come. At the end of the battle, the river was red with the blood of the Zulus; hence the Blood River. The Whites had won.

May I interject here and say that this, at its very core, was not a battle between Black and White . . . it was a battle between the God of the Covenant and the forefather spirits and gods of the Zulus. It was a battle between the only living God and dead man-made gods. Truth is, the living

God does not distinguish between color or creed. Only people in their corruptible, carnal, self-centered ways and thinking do that. If only the Whites had comprehended this truth back then.

The Zulus accepted defeat and a long journey of building and establishing a country and accommodating the different nations started. The Whites kept their promise to the God of the Covenant, and God blessed them, allowing them to prosper greatly in a country where they were the minority. When I was growing up, there were nine Black nationalities and two White nationalities living in South Africa.

In the eyes of the White Afrikaner leaders who first established apartheid, apartheid was supposed to be a very noble act of empowerment for the Black tribal people and protection for the White people. The White Afrikaners, who were first-world Westerners, considered themselves further developed than the third-world Black African tribal people. They considered themselves educated and refined as opposed to the Black tribal people who were, according to their Western standards, barbaric and primitive and uneducated. They were also afraid of more "blood rivers."

The idea of allowing Black tribal children to mingle with White Afrikaner children in schools and playgrounds felt threatening and wrong to the Westerners. And furthermore, the cultural differences just didn't lend themselves to socializing together in public spaces. The "barbaric" mannerisms of the Black tribal people were insulting to the sensitivities of the "refined" White Afrikaner people. There was also fear, an emotion cutting deep to the core because of the bloody fights of the past.

Apartheid or segregation was supposed to create separate environments where the White Westerners and their children could continue to develop at their educated pace while the primitive Black African tribal people and their children could slowly be brought up to Western standards, through separate education and developmental programs. This would protect White Westerners from the so-called barbarisms of uneducated Black tribal people, while it offered the Black tribal people the opportunity to play catch up in their own environment at their own pace. It sounded honorable at the time, but was it really? I'll leave that up to you, the reader, to decide.

It is also worth mentioning that apartheid wasn't just enforced between Whites and Blacks. My dad worked on the gold mines, and the mines built hostels to accommodate their Black workers; they had to separate the Xhosas and the Zulus in the hostels to avoid bloody confrontations. Nobody would or seemingly could get along, and so apartheid or segregation seemed like an obvious, viable solution. It seemed like a reasonable governmental solution to a very complex social problem. Did I mention that Government can only manage hearts through rules and regulations, it can't change hearts?

Furthermore, the devil is always in the details. Apartheid became a tool for White self-exaltation and White supremacy, leading to oppression and murder. It empowered and entitled the White Afrikaner, while literally enslaving the Black tribal people, keeping them suppressed, poor, impoverished and at the mercy of their White bosses. And before anybody judges the White Afrikaner . . . just about every country in this world has a similar history of one nation oppressing another in the struggle for self-preservation, self-exaltation and supremacy.

The spirit of pharaoh is everywhere! Even God's children succumb to the spirit of pharaoh when they replace God and His values with their own vices. In South Africa, the White Afrikaner, who worshipped the God of the Covenant, was actually persuaded by religious and political leaders alike that apartheid was Biblical and therefore God's will. These were leaders using God and Scripture to manipulate the masses in order to secure supremacy. And the White Afrikaner masses followed their leaders because of their own prejudiced ignorance and the great benefit to their lifestyle. They were blinded by their prejudice and their own sense of empowerment. What they didn't realize was, they themselves were being manipulated and used by the spirit of pharaoh and in the process set up for a fall in the spiritual world, because, even though they as a nation still worshipped the God of the Covenant on the outside, on the inside, in their hearts, they gradually started relying on their own twisted version of the Word and their own exalted sense of prejudice.

Pharaoh and his followers, in the story of Exodus, was being set up for a fall.

"Come, let us deal wisely with them, or else they will multiply and in the event of war, they will also join themselves to those who hate us, and fight against us and depart from the land." – Exodus 1:10

When Pharaoh looked at the nation of Israel, he did not see Joseph and the God of the Covenant, he saw a nation that was increasing in numbers at an alarming pace and outnumbering the Egyptians. He foresaw the possibility of Israel siding with an enemy during a time of war and over-powering Egypt. He felt threatened by the sheer size of Israel as a people; but, interestingly enough, he didn't want them to leave Egypt.

Even though he felt threatened by them, he recognized that their strength and might could be channeled to Egypt's advantage, if managed properly. In his mind, they could be used as cheap labor to develop Egypt's infrastructure and real estate. He considered them a valuable but risky economic asset, so he wanted to keep them; but, he realized that he needed to manage the risk aggressively.

His risk management approach was to control their numbers by killing the baby boys and to control their mindset by using force and harsh slavery to keep them submissive. He decided to create a slavery mindset amongst them. I find it interesting that till this very day; slavery is one of the most lucrative industries in the world. The devil's method has never changed.

The God of the Covenant teaches us through Scripture to subdue the "earth," not people. People with Pharaoh's mindset end up subduing and controlling other people, which is not Scriptural. Scripture commands us to love and find ways to accommodate people.

The Israelites become Pharaoh's slaves.

"And they built for Pharaoh storage cities, Pithom and Raamses." –
Exodus 1:11

The irony of this story is, even though the people of Israel were more and mightier than the Egyptians, according to Exodus 1:9, they submitted to the oppressive political ideology of Pharaoh. They allowed themselves and their children to be pushed into forced labor and slavery by the laws of the land imposed by this new Pharaoh. They were used to living in the aftermath of a good Pharaoh who acknowledged the God of the Covenant and His servant, Joseph. The blessing was still being enjoyed by both Israelites and Egyptians, but the acknowledgment of the God of the Covenant had been erased, making them gullible to forces of darkness and complacency. Humanity without God leads to corruption and suffering.

The new Pharaoh's oppressive laws blinded Israel to their true potential and God-designed calling and obliterated the memory of the God of the Covenant and Joseph. They had two advantages they could have leveraged in a heartbeat, if they hadn't been so blind. One was obvious: they outnumbered the Egyptians. Two should have been obvious as well; they belonged to the God of the Covenant. They had a double advantage over the Egyptians, but they chose to submit to slavery and harsh, cruel forced labor instead.

What would have happened if they had said no to this oppressive law of the new Pharaoh? Would Pharaoh have been willing to negotiate and change his mind? Would the God of the Covenant have intervened and worked in their favor? We will never know, because by harshly oppressing them, the Pharaoh used an age-old method to keep the masses submissive—it's called fear. The truth is, Pharaoh himself was acting out of fear. Fear begets fear.

Somewhere along the line, Israel's fear of God was replaced by a fear of the Pharaoh, so they embraced a "slavery mindset."

A slavery mindset still holds God's children captive today.
"Concerning Him [Jesus] we have much to say, and it is hard to explain, since you have become dull of hearing. For though by this time you ought to be teachers, you have need again for someone to teach you the elementary principles of the oracles of God, and you have come to need milk and not solid food. For everyone who partakes only of milk is not accustomed to the world of righteousness, for he is an infant." – Hebrews 5:11-13

Besides the fact that Christians are being persecuted and even murdered all around the world because of their Christian values and belief in Jesus Christ, it's upsetting to see how many Christians in the free world, the western world, are subdued and enslaved by work, money, possessions, manipulative people, ideologies, hang-ups, debt, divorce, pornography, and the list goes on. The spirit of pharaoh still enslaves and kills by using our human lusts, desires, hang-ups and prejudices against us.

Satan tickles and tempts our carnal natures and desires until we become our own biggest enemy. Christians are tripping over themselves and their environments all the time, hardly ever reaching their full potential in the kingdom of Christ, yours truly included. In so doing, most Christians are rendered powerless and oppressed, even though they profess Jesus, the King of the Universe, as their Savior. Spiritually, they're going to heaven; but on earth, they're not worth diddly-squat to the kingdom. Mission accomplished by the spirit of pharaoh, satan himself!

Paul refers to these Christians in Hebrews 5:11-13, who sadly seem to comprise a large portion of the Christian church today, as follows, *"Concerning Him [Jesus] we have much to say, and it is hard to explain, since you have become dull of hearing. For though by this time you ought to be teachers, you have need again for someone to teach you the elementary principles of the oracles of God, and you have come to need milk and not solid food. For everyone who partakes only of milk is not accustomed to the world of righteousness, for he is an infant."*

All the spirit of pharaoh has to achieve, is to keep Christians in the infant stage where they remain slaves to carnality and to life and are therefore no different to the average Joe or Jane next door. This renders them powerless for kingdom victories on the earth, keeping corruption and mediocrity on the cutting edge of society. Infants have no influence in society. As a matter of fact, infants are at the mercy of society!

Many Christians talk the talk, but very few walk the walk. Those who walk the walk are described by Paul as follows in Hebrews 5:14: *"Solid food is for the mature, who because of practice have their senses trained to discern good and evil."*

For the most part, the church either "babysits" or "country clubs" and does not raise practicing, discerning, mature people of faith who have been proved obedient and made perfect through their suffering/temptations. *"Although He [Jesus] was a Son, He learned obedience from the things which He suffered. And having been made perfect, He [Jesus] became . . . the source of eternal salvation"* (Hebrews 5:8).

Jesus became the source of salvation, because He practiced obedience even in the midst of great trials and tribulations and peer pressure. His kingdom power was activated and made perfect through His obedience. Today, the church has too many disobedient, shallow, whiny babies who have never reached the level of Holy Spirit excellence that can unleash kingdom power in and through themselves. Is it possible that even the so called "mature" are still tripping over too many degrees of their carnal natures, giving the spirit of pharaoh permission to harass and enslave them and their communities, limiting their kingdom power?

Allow me to paraphrase some of Stephen R Covey's thoughts in the next couple of paragraphs, which can be found in his book called, *Principle-Centered Leadership*[1]. These thoughts have comingled with mine over the years, so I'm not quite sure anymore where his ends and mine begins, but I want to submit that a "slavery mindset," if I understand

---

[1] Stephen R Covey, Principle Centered Leadership (Simon & Schuster New York, 1992)

Covey correctly, is designed to paralyze us by suppressing our creativity, confidence, self-esteem and true potential, turning us into reactive instead of secure, stable, creative individuals. It keeps us submissive to the anxieties and pressures of life. A slavery mindset causes us to repeat mistakes because we don't overcome. It causes us to be emotionally dependent on others because we're not secure in ourselves. It causes us to follow trends instead of create them. We tend to be a reflection of external conditions and internal moods, which change moment by moment. Reactive people are slaves to their physical, emotional, social and political environment.

Are you reactive to people and your environment, or are you secure within yourself? Do you, like Pharaoh, measure your success by people's opinions, numerical statistics and the success of your competition? Or are you able to hold the course and stay secure in the midst of downturns, negative feedback and others overtaking you? Are you constantly trying to dominate your space? Are you constantly blaming other people and circumstances for the condition you're in? Is it always somebody else's fault, your spouse maybe, or a co-worker, boss, the government, society or your ex? Are you constantly in panic mode? Are you always making changes in order to please other people and to keep up with the latest trends?

Look around you. How many incomplete tasks are surrounding you—things you started but never finished—reminders of your good intentions but inability to follow through to completion? Why didn't you finish them? You are a slave to whoever/whatever controls you!

Do you have a slavery mindset (reactive) or a pharaoh mindset (manipulative) or a Joseph mindset (principle-centered immersed in a personal relationship with the living God)?

Bear in mind that sometimes we interchange these mindsets depending on the situation in which we find ourselves. The truth is, we all indulge in slavery and pharaoh mindsets, but few explore the Joseph mindset. These mindsets are no respecter of persons and are found in all walks of life, whether rich or poor, male or female, black or white; it makes no difference.

Analyze every compartment of your life and try to identify which mindset reigns in that compartment. Ask Holy Spirit to illuminate the corridors and rooms of your heart with His revelation.

The goal is to let Holy Spirit identify and annihilate the slavery and pharaoh mindsets in our lives and show us how to embrace and start practicing a true, consistent Joseph mindset in every situation throughout every aspect of our lives. And as a people full of Holy Spirit, we also need to recognize the slavery and pharaoh mindsets motivating others so that we don't fall prey to their vices. The spirit of pharaoh will use other people and people groups to trip us up if we are not vigilant and in true relationship with the living God of the Covenant.

Our goal should be to become a Joseph in our environment, irrespective of our physical position in society, bringing the God of the Covenant and His supernatural solutions to the table we call life, *"with gentleness correcting those who are in opposition, if perhaps God may grant them repentance leading to the knowledge of the truth, and they may come to their senses and escape from the snare of the devil, having been held captive by him to do his will"* (2 Timothy 2:25-26).

The midwives understood and practiced the "Joseph mindset."

"But the midwives feared God and did not do as the king of Egypt [Pharaoh] had commanded them but let the boys live. So God was good to the midwives . . . Because the midwives feared God, He established households for them." – Exodus 1:17, 20-21

Most commentaries teach that fearing God is to have reverential trust or reverential respect. These terms, however, downplay the true meaning. We can reverentially trust or respect someone, but still respectfully disagree on certain issues and therefore still choose to do our own thing when it comes to those issues. No, to fear God means exactly what it says: "fear." Paul reminds us of God's discipline in Hebrews 12: 5 and 6 where he writes, *"My son, do not regard lightly the discipline of the Lord, nor faint when you are reproved by Him; for those whom the Lord loves He disciplines, and He scourges every son whom He receives."*

Today, in too many churches, God has been watered down to just another friend down the road whom we visit and listen to on Sunday while we go about our own business Monday through Saturday. This same Sunday culture makes its followers and society think that the Bible is open for all kinds of different interpretations and, therefore, so is God.

Too many Christians have become academic pharisees, studying and twisting the Word to suit personal agendas, often leaving God, who is the Author of the Word, out of the equation. Church is often an academic relationship with the Bible instead of an active, vibrant, personal and also fearful relationship with Yahweh, who is God the Father, God the Son and God the Holy Spirit.

Christians also often take the concept of grace and use it as an excuse to live unholy, sinful lives whilst quoting that wonderful verse in the Bible that says we *"all fall short of the glory of God"* (Romans 3:23). Wow! What an excuse to sin and excuse other people's sins! And, by the way, a debate is currently floating around that asks the question, what exactly is sin? You see, the minute you define sin, you have to have knowledge of right and wrong. In today's society, however, in the current debate, your wrong might be my right, which leaves the Bible open for interpretation. I'll interpret it the way I want to, and you interpret it the way you want to. That's what happens when people serve a book? Words are easily twisted and adapted to establish new truths.

The Western church has a problem: there is no fear of and personal relationship with the God of "the Book." God has been watered down to a pal you hang out with instead of *the* Sovereign God you approach on your knees. The church also has no fear for the consequences of disobeying God.

When the midwives had to choose between disobeying Pharaoh and disobeying God, they didn't hesitate because they understood sin and its consequences. They were willing to risk their lives to disobey Pharaoh because they feared God much more than they feared Pharaoh.

The Apostle Paul writes in Philippians 2:12 that each child of the living God should work out their personal salvation "with *fear* and trembling". Interpreting the Bible and living God's principles in and through an active relationship with Him, from His heart and His mind, my friend, is no sterile, academic, left-open-for-interpretation exercise. It is literally a matter of life or death. Only when you approach God and His Word with fear and trembling can you responsibly converse with the Word through His Holy Spirit and learn to hear His voice accurately, because *fear* and *trembling* takes away arrogant opinions and replaces them with humbleness and receptivity. And it's only in that place of humbleness and receptivity that we are invited deeper into a place of intimacy and love. Only then does He become Father God.

Solomon states in Proverbs 3:7 "*Do not be wise in your own eyes; fear the Lord.*" And the Psalmist says in Psalm 147:10 and 11, "*He [God] does not delight in the strength of the horse; He does not take pleasure in the legs of a man. The Lord favors those who fear Him, those who wait for His lovingkindness.*"

I asked the question earlier. What would have happened if the Israelites had feared God and said no to the new, harsh slavery laws of the Pharaoh? And if it wasn't possible to say no, what would have happened if they had put their trust in God whilst submitting to the harsh treatment of the Pharaoh instead of operating from a place of inferiority and fear of man? Based on what happened to the midwives, I think we can safely assume they would have enjoyed God's favor. They certainly would have faced challenges based on what we know about this Pharaoh and his hardheadedness, but God would have worked that out.

Paul teaches us in I Corinthians 10:13, "*No temptation has overtaken you but such as is common to man; and God is faithful, who will not allow you to be tempted beyond what you are able, but with the temptation will provide the way of escape also, so that you will be able to endure."* We are able to grasp and hear this truth only when we are fully immersed in a personal relationship with Father God. Israel, at the time, was not.

In summary, the Joseph mindset which embraces the fear of the Lord and enters into a beautiful, intimate relationship with the living God of the Covenant attracts blessing into your life, giving you a stable, prosperous home base (Father God's heart) from which to work, so that you can face and overcome the challenges life throws at you. A great example in this story is God blessing the midwives by establishing households for them.

Both the slavery and the pharaoh mindset however, attract defeat into your life, robbing you of stability and therefore eroding all other aspects of life as well. This is a natural law just like the law of gravity. You may be able to temporarily circumvent it, but eventually the curse will catch up with you.

"But the humble will inherit the land and will delight themselves in abundant prosperity." – Psalm 36:11

CHAPTER 2

The Joseph Mindset Requires Conviction

"It was at this time that Moses was born; and he was lovely in the sight of God." – Acts 7:20

"The woman conceived and bore a son; and when she saw that he was beautiful, she hid him for three months." – Exodus 2:2

At the time of this writing, my brother and his wife had given birth to premature twins, a boy and a girl. It was a difficult journey, but the reward was sweet. My brother has a way of pinning down his dog and kissing him all over; well, according to reports, he was doing the same to his adorable newborn babies. He couldn't stop holding and kissing them.

I don't have children, but I do have two adorable puppy dogs—actually they're adults, but they'll always be puppies to me. I often look at them and wonder just how much fun God, our Creator, must have had creating them? I mean, how do you create "adorable" and not have warm fuzzies all over? I understand totally what the writer, inspired by Holy Spirit, was trying to convey in Genesis 1 when he wrote that every time, after God created a theme, *"God saw that it was good."* I can just imagine our Creator standing back, gazing at the "adorable" that He just created and getting warm fuzzies all over.

Warm fuzzies and faith-filled conviction germinate a seed of salvation.

"The woman conceived and bore a son; and when she saw that he was beautiful, she hid him for three months. But when she could hide him no longer, [faith-filled conviction] . . . got him a wicker basket and covered it over with tar and pitch." – Exodus 2:3

We read that Moses was *"lovely in the sight of God"* (Acts 7:20). Moses wasn't just good, he was lovely! He definitely gave God "warm fuzzies" all over and some. Moses was given an anointing, a beautiful spiritual mantle which he would wear and minister from as Israel's deliverer, whilst leading the nation out of the slavery bondage of Egypt, through the wilderness, to the Promised Land. Moses' mother must have recognized this anointing as we read, *"She saw that he was beautiful"* (Exodus 2:2). Safe to say, Moses gave his mother warm fuzzies too.

She sensed something special about Moses; some kind of divine countenance. The reason I say this is, just about all the Hebrew parents in this story must have found their babies to be beautiful—most parents do. So, for the writer to use it as the main reason for the parents to hide Moses, this must have been a beauty that went beyond the normal "oohs" and "aahs."

Moses beauty apparently prompted his parents to go to extreme lengths to hide their newborn from a raging Pharaoh who was bent on murdering every little Hebrew baby boy and being quite successful in his killing spree. Stephen describes in Acts 7:19 how the fathers were mistreated, even tortured, until they gave up their baby sons to be thrown in the Nile and drowned (Exodus 1:22). It was a heart-wrenching time of woeful loss and heartless, relentless abuse and murder. The fact that they could even hide her pregnancy (my assumption) and then hide the newborn baby for three months is a miracle in itself.

This story reminds me of another time in Israel's history when "*a voice was heard in Ramah, weeping and great mourning, Rachel weeping for her children; and she refused to be comforted, because they were no more*" (Matthew 2:18). This happened when Herod realized that the magi had tricked him. Instead of returning to Herod to disclose the place where the child Jesus was, they left by a different route so as to avoid Herod. When he realized that they had left without reporting to him, he became enraged and also went on a killing spree. He had all male children who were in Bethlehem up to the age of two years old slain, hoping one of them would be the child Jesus, the one whom he thought could potentially take his throne. Sounds a lot like Pharaoh, doesn't it? Different leader, same spirit.

As I discussed in the previous chapter, the spirit of pharaoh has been everywhere throughout the ages. Revelation 12:12 actually reveals this spirit to us: "*Woe to the earth and the sea, because the devil has come down to you, having great wrath, knowing that he has only a short time.*" Paul warns us against this spirit in Ephesians 6:10-12: "*Finally, be strong in the Lord and in the strength of His might. Put on the full armor of God, so that you will be able to stand firm against the schemes of the devil. For our struggle is not against flesh and blood, but against the rulers, against the powers, against the world forces of this darkness, against the spiritual forces of wickedness in the heavenly places.*"

Moses parents didn't have the book of Revelations or Ephesians as their guide, but they had a Joseph mindset and therefore feared God more than they feared Pharaoh. Just like the midwives and Joseph before them, they too understood the principle of faith we read about in Hebrews 11:23 and Ephesians 6:10-12. Their faith was apparently just as persistent and relentless as Pharaoh's resolve to kill Hebrew baby boys.

They demonstrated a level of faith that goes beyond lip service, beyond doubts, beyond physical and mental and geographical limitations, beyond circumstances, beyond the naysayers. They demonstrated a faith that simply and profoundly believed that God is—period. God is! Nobody else came close.

So, when it became impossible to hide Moses anymore, this faith-filled conviction *"got him a wicker basket and covered it over with tar and pitch. Then . . . put the child into it and set it among the reeds by the bank of the Nile . . . [then] stood at a distance to find out what would happen to him"* (Exodus 2:3-4).

A most extraordinary thing happened.
"The daughter of Pharaoh came down to bathe at the Nile . . . and she saw the basket among the reeds and sent her maid, and she brought it to her." – Exodus 2:5

Only one person in the whole of Egypt could publicly go against the Pharaoh's edict to kill all Hebrew baby boys and get away with it—daddy's little girl—the princess. You can read the whole story in Exodus 2:5-10.

Never in a million years would a Hebrew slave have thought of, or got away with, approaching her and asking her to adopt and protect their baby boy; but God could, and did.

And so a seed of redemption, called by God to lead His people out of Egypt, is born/germinated. Initially he is protected by the faith-filled conviction of his parents, and then, through Divine intervention, he is put in protective custody under the care of the princess, away from the murderous hunt of Pharaoh.

God really does make a way where there seems to be no way. *"For My thoughts are not your thoughts, neither are your ways My ways', declares the Lord"* (Isaiah 55:8).

Faith-filled conviction germinates the seed of a new nation.
"With the power of their firearms and with their ox wagons in a laager formation and some excellent tactics, the Boers fought off the Zulu." – J.G. Bantjes[2]

On Sunday 16 December 1838, approximately 460 Boer men, led by Andries Pretorius, representing a group of people that would later be called the "Afrikaner," faced an enemy of approximately twenty to thirty thousand Zulu men on the bank of the Ncome River in what is today called KwaZulu-Natal, South Africa. According to some history books, Andries Pretorius and his men were outnumbered about 60 to 1, maybe more. Even though the precise numbers are debatable, all historians agree that they were heavily outnumbered. It would require a miracle for them to survive, let alone win the battle.

J.G. Bantjes, Andries Pretorius's secretary, describes in his journal how, on Sunday December 9, 1838, the Boers gathered together outside in a clearing to have church. During this church service, they took a vow which became known as the "Day of the Vow or Covenant" in which they promised God that, should He give them the victory, they would build a church as "a memorial of His Great Name at a place where it shall please Him." This congregation would later become part of a cooperate entity called the Dutch Reformed Church.

During this church service, they also asked God to help them accomplish the vow after they defeated the Zulus and promised to commemorate the Day of the Vow as a Sabbath every year for all generations to come, raising their children in the awareness of this Almighty God and His mighty act of redemption on that day.

Before the battle, the Zulu warriors also attended their own ceremonies. Wikipedia quotes the South African Department of Art and Culture's statement, "In ceremonies that lasted about three days, 'izinyanga zempi,' specialist war doctors, prepared 'izinteleze' medicines which made warriors invincible in the face of their opponents."

---

[2] Battle of Blood River (Wikipedia The Free Encyclopedia, Google)

It's worth repeating that what set these two groups apart was not their ethnicity, language, background, level of education or development, power and might . . . it wasn't anything like that—although all those differences did exist at the time. What set them apart was this: the Boers put their faith in the God of the Covenant, while the Zulus put their faith in their specialist war doctors and medicines based on forefather spiritual traditions and gods.

Wikipedia states, "With the power of their firearms and with their ox wagons in a laager formation and some excellent tactics, the Boers fought off the Zulu. After three hours, the Boers had killed an estimated three thousand Zulu soldiers and had only three of their men wounded, among them Pretorius . . . The Zulu withdrew in defeat, many crossing the river which had turned red with blood and was thereafter known as the Battle of Blood River."

This small group of Boers, like Moses parents, demonstrated a level of faith that goes beyond lip service, beyond doubts, beyond physical and mental and geographical limitations, beyond circumstances, beyond the naysayers—they demonstrated a faith that simply and profoundly believed that God is—period. God is! Nobody else comes close.

And so the seed was planted on a land that would later be called South Africa, for a nation to be born that should have been a testimony of God's great and wonderful works, making God disciples of the other nations that co-existed with them; but sadly they missed God's highest for South Africa.

Could it be that we need to evaluate the Battle of Blood River through God's eyes, not racial eyes? *"For My thoughts are not your thoughts, neither are your ways My ways', declares the Lord"* (Isaiah 55:8).

Faith-filled conviction germinates a new calling.

On a Sunday morning in 1982 or 1983, I was standing in a Dutch Reformed Church building as a high school teenager worshiping God when I looked at the pulpit, and my heart suddenly started racing as a calling materialized. In that moment, I felt an overwhelming desire to stand on a pulpit in the Dutch Reformed Church and preach; over the months that followed, that desire, that calling, grew louder and louder.

I didn't dare to express it verbally because, at the time, women were not allowed on the pulpit of the Dutch Reformed Church. A woman pastor was considered heresy! Women could do missionary work in the mission fields, but they could not pastor a Dutch Reformed Church in South Africa. Besides, ever since I was five years old, I had wanted to be a medical doctor. Everybody was expecting me to become a doctor.

I tried to persist in my goal to become a doctor, but the more I tried to persist, the more things deteriorated. It became more and more difficult for me to study, personal relationships became strained, my grades started declining and eventually I entered university with a less-than-acceptable high school grade for med school. Bottom line, I wasn't accepted, but was allowed into a Medical Science Degree (B Med Sc.) with the plan to use this degree as a bridge to get into med school. However, that didn't work out either.

I was learning that being disobedient to a specific calling from God is like banging your head against a brick wall. For the most part, God gives us free will; but in some instances, He drafts people. I was one of those people. Nothing else worked out for me. I could not concentrate for even ten minutes on my studies without feeling the room close in on me and my breath being squeezed out of me. I would have to flee from my desk. I was desperately trying to hang in there to get at least passing grades the first semester at university. However, the more desperate I became, the less I could study. With the approaching semester exams looming, I knew I was toast. As a matter of fact, I was already starting to think about a life in the work force without any degree.

I'm not quite sure what transpired next. I'll try to describe it as best I can remember. It was evening, and my roommate and I were studying in our dormitory room when an announcement came over the intercom system. It was a male first-year student asking if any of the first-year girls—we lived in a girls-only dormitory—owned a vehicle. First-year students were not allowed to have vehicles on campus unless authorized. He was bored and wanted to go to the movies.

I was the only first-year student in the dormitory who had a vehicle, and you guessed it, all of a sudden just about the whole flank where I lived wanted to go to the movies. You can just imagine what my car looked like, packed with who knows how many first-year students going to the movie theater. The male student sat next to me in the front, while all the girls were piled up on each other's laps in the back. I had one of those old long, rectangular Datsuns.

As I'm driving down the road, he introduces himself and tells me he's currently studying agriculture but . . . drum roll, please . . . he has this calling from God to become a pastor in the Dutch Reformed Church. Was God setting me up?

After much wrestling, he said, he had decided that he was going to the administrative offices the next morning to change his course. He was going to start a bachelor's degree in theology, which was the first of two degrees required in order to become a pastor in the Dutch Reformed Church.

You can call it stupidity, call it spontaneity, call it desperation, call it answering God's call—my parents had other names for it, which I can't repeat. After all, I was only eighteen years old at the time and still under their care. Call it teenager foolishness, whatever you want to call it, what happened next just happened. Before I had time to analyze what I was doing, I looked at him and said, "I'm going with you in the morning." My only excuse was, "God set me up!"

I walked out of the administrative offices the next morning with my new friend, both of us holding our new class rosters in our hands, full of excitement, but I also had absolutely no idea how I was going to break the news to my parents. I had not shared my calling with them—ever! And, women were not allowed to be pastors in the Dutch Reformed Church! I'll leave it up to your imagination as to how my parents took the news.

Was I running away from failing grades or was I answering God's call? Was God intervening just in time, or was I using God as a scapegoat?

My resolve and the answer to the above questions and ultimately my faith-filled conviction would be tested and retested and tested some more in the years that followed. It took me nine years to complete the two degrees I needed to become a pastor in the Dutch Reformed Church. The first degree took me six years, part time, while I supported myself by working as a teller in a bank by day, attending class by night and studying over the weekends. Then it took another three years, full-time, to complete my second degree, which included the Dutch Reformed Seminary.

In the eighth year of my studies, the Dutch Reformed Church finally opened its pulpits to women and allowed women to be ordained as pastors! All this time, I had been studying based on a faith-filled conviction that God had called me to pastor in a Dutch Reformed congregation without any evidence that it would or could ever happen. God was germinating a seed of His calling in and through me, and I would be and still am slowly and clumsily learning how to demonstrate a level of faith that goes beyond lip service, beyond doubts, beyond physical and mental and geographical limitations, beyond circumstances, beyond the naysayers. I would, through an excruciating process, learn about a faith that simply and profoundly believes that God is—period.

I would learn about Hebrews 11:6, which says, *"For he who comes to God must believe that He is and that He is a rewarder of those who seek Him."* I would learn about Romans 8:31, which declares, *"If God is for us, who can be against us?"* And ultimately, many years later, I would start scratching at the surface of John 15:7, which promises, *"If you abide in Me, and My words abide in you, ask whatever you wish, and it will be done for you."*

Above all, I would learn that faith-filled conviction is not for the fainthearted.

The kind of faith demonstrated by Moses' parents and the reward promised in John 15:7 is available to all God's children in and through Jesus Christ, but the execution of it (obedience, Deuteronomy 28:1; belief, Hebrews

11:6; abiding; John 15:7) is not for the fainthearted. We all get salvation on the platter of the Cross, but, once saved, the journey of faith comes at great cost. Kathryn Kuhlman, one of the greatest evangelists and healers of all times, once said that it cost her everything.

In my introduction to this book, I gave a simplified comparison between the blessing and the curse. I purposely described it with the word *simplified* because, in reality, it takes fearful and trembling conviction to live the kind of faith that attracts the fullness of the blessing we read about in Deuteronomy 28:1-14. There is nothing simple about it. I once heard Bill Johnson preach that it requires all of us in exchange for all of God.

Through different levels of faith and even human ability, we can annex little pockets of the blessing column for short periods of time; but the process of actually attracting the fullness of the complete blessing column, which leads us to living in the fruition of John 15:7, is not for the fainthearted. The journey to get to the fruition of John 15:7 is daunting. Bill Johnson writes in his book, *Hosting the Presence,* that *"hosting God is filled with honor and pleasure, cost and mystery."*[3]

Many of God's children deprive themselves of the honor and pleasure of hosting God, because they choose to remain infants in their faith. They are baffled and daunted by and often ignorant of the cost and the mystery of abiding in Christ, and therefore they live their entire lives struggling with the repercussions of different degrees of the curse as described in Deuteronomy 28:15-68. Even people who are well on their way into the heart of John 15:7 are affected by the repercussions of this curse, because of people around them making decisions that attract the curse.

The reward of the curse is terrible, but it's the road of least resistance. It's easier to submit to the spirit of pharaoh and harbor and nurture pharaoh and slavery mindsets, often even for the average Christian professing Jesus Christ as their Savior. Too many times, Christians profess, "We're heading for heaven, folks," but their lifestyle is that of fear and anxiety and

---

[3] Bill Johnson, Hosting the Presence (Destiny Image Publishes, Inc. 2012), 29

often defeat on this earth, far below what God intended for His children. Can we really blame non-Christians for steering clear of a hypocritical church based on a twisted, self-serving weak version of the Bible?

There is a place in Christ where you can ask whatever you wish.

"If you abide in Me, and My words abide in you, ask whatever you wish, and it will be done for you." – John 15:7

According to John, a place of intimacy in Christ, in this lifetime, on this earth, is available to all God's children, where you can ask whatever you wish and it will be done. Some church denominations water this down to a shallow "name it and claim it" prosperity theology, as if things are just going to fall in your lap, and others theologize it completely away; but I believe it is relevant and available for every Christian today in its unadulterated form as written in John 15. The reason I believe this place in Christ still exists today is because it has been revealed to us through Scripture: *"The things revealed belong to us and to our sons [children] forever"* (Deuteronomy 29:29).

John 15:7 is part of our revealed heritage forever, and I believe a generation of Christians will, just like the generation of Joshua and Caleb, enter their Promised Land called the kingdom of Christ. They will enter into this revealed heritage of John 15 and live from it through a personal relationship with Holy Spirit, before the coming of Jesus Christ. Jesus said He was coming for a church *"in all her glory, having no spot or wrinkle or any such thing"* (Ephesians 5:27). John 15 describes that generation of the church.

Until such an entire church generation arises, however, I believe, this truth is available to every individual who accepts Christ as their Savior and who is willing to pursue it. If you have accepted Jesus Christ as your personal Savior, you hold the seed to this promise in your hand and your faith holds the ability to loose the Power to germinate and cultivate and ultimately eat and distribute the fruit of it through your relationship with Holy Spirit and your willingness to yield to the journey. Few have received or understood the conviction to travel to that place in Christ, and even fewer have embraced the conviction to stay.

Are you prepared to yield to the journey and pursue that place in Christ as depicted by John 15? Are you prepared to trust God to keep you safe along the way? Are you prepared to risk all of you for all of God? Are you willing to pursue a level of faith that goes beyond lip service, beyond doubts, beyond physical and mental and geographical limitations, beyond circumstances, beyond the naysayers? Are you willing to pursue a place in Christ that simply and profoundly believes that God is—period? God is! No more excuses.

Let me remind you, the journey there is hard, but I will prove to you through the pages of this book that the reward is sweet!

"So we conclude that there is still a full and complete rest waiting for Believers to experience. As we enter into God's faith-rest life we cease from our own works, just as God celebrates His finished works and rests in them. So then we must give our all and be eager to experience this faith-rest life, so that no one falls short by following the same pattern of doubt and unbelief." – Hebrews 4:9-11, AMP

CHAPTER 3

When A Calling Seems Paradoxical

"Now it came about in those days, when Moses had grown up, that he went out to his brethren." – Exodus 2:11

"By faith Moses, when he had grown up, refused to be called the son of Pharaoh's daughter, choosing rather to endure ill-treatment with the people of God than to enjoy the passing pleasures of sin, considering the reproach of Christ greater riches than the treasures of Egypt; for he was looking to the reward." – Hebrews 11:24-26

"And without faith it is impossible to please Him, for he who comes to God must believe that He is and that He is a rewarder of those who seek Him." – Hebrews 11:5

A calling is born

Apparently Moses' mother, who acted as Moses' nanny after he was adopted by the Egyptian princess, did a good job teaching Moses about the God of the Covenant. According to Paul in Hebrews 11, Moses embraced the teachings of this Covenant God and His people by choosing to serve God and identify with God's people, the Hebrew slaves.

Paul also gives us insight into the fact that Moses had quite an advanced revelation of Christ for the time in which he lived. He writes about Moses, *"Considering the reproach of Christ greater riches than the treasures of Egypt; for he was looking to the reward"* (Hebrew 11:26). Where did Moses get this revelation?

It's obvious that his parents had a deep relationship with God and that they must have shared their knowledge of God and possibly the coming Messiah with him, but according to Paul, Moses' relationship with God went even deeper. Moses had a revelation of Christ Himself, that He is a rewarder of those who seek Him and according to Paul, Moses wanted the reward. This kind of revelation, which was far ahead of his peers, could have come only through his own personal, intimate times of worship and relationship with God. In other words, God Himself must have revealed this to Moses.

I say this because during my own personal, intimate times with God, I find that there are layers and layers of intimacy within God; and He allows us to peel back those layers through worship and personal relationship with Him. Every new layer of intimacy we enter into introduces us to a greater revelation of the knowledge of God. Paul actually prays for the Ephesians, *"that the God of our Lord Jesus Christ, the Father of glory, may give to you a spirit of wisdom and of revelation in the knowledge of Him,"* and it is that spirit of revelation that helps us go deeper and deeper. I believe every layer unveils and makes available new dimensions of knowledge of God and rewards in Christ, with John 15 being the ultimate reward once an individual enters the ultimate layer or dimension of abiding in Christ through Holy Spirit.

Moses was definitely pursuing God, and God had already allowed him to start peeling back some layers, introducing him to a dimension of Christ that his peers had not seen or grasped yet. I believe, not even the riches and privileges of Egypt could sway him from his pursuit of God after he had tasted Christ and gotten a glimpse of the reward.

I remember the first time Jesus revealed Himself to me, giving me a taste of a reward called "His friendship" which we read about in John 15:15. I had just experienced what felt like a devastating experience for a ninth grader. I was lying in my bed that night after the incident, crying and crying and crying. At one point, I almost sobbed out aloud, "I wish I had a friend." I felt so alone, so isolated, so misunderstood and unloved in that moment. All of a sudden, I was aware of a Presence in the far corner of my bedroom, close to the window, and in the same moment I heard an impression in my mind, "I'll be your Friend." I can't explain it, but I knew instantly that it was Jesus, and I instantly embraced Him as my Lord and Savior . . . and He became my Friend.

John 15:15 states, *"No longer do I call you slaves, for the slave does not know what his master is doing; but I have called you friends, for all things that I have heard from My Father I have made known to you."*

In the preface of this book, I describe how, starting at the age of six, I became aware of someone or something tugging at my spirit. All of a sudden, in that moment in my bedroom, I finally came to know who it was . . . it was Jesus! That someone or something that I had been pursuing or, better said, who had been pursuing me, finally revealed Himself to me as my Redeemer, Jesus Christ—my Friend! It would be years before Jesus would visit me again, but nothing could ever sway me from Jesus after that encounter with Him. So, based on my personal experience, it wouldn't surprise me at all if Moses had an encounter with Jesus, the Christ.

Anyway, we do know for certain, according to Paul, that he somehow identified with Christ, who is a rewarder of those who seek Him; and we know from Paul's writings that he felt the heart of God for the plight of

God's people. Moses' heart was already being stirred in the direction of redemption for the Hebrew slaves.

So, who is Moses at this point? Moses is the adopted son of an Egyptian princess, an Egyptian prince, raised in a very privileged, educated, well-groomed way, right in the center of the enemy's camp, learning the enemy's language, culture and rules of engagement. He is also the son of Hebrew slaves who were mercilessly mistreated and abused. He is also a child of the Covenant God with a heart for righteousness and the plight of God's children. He also has a much deeper revelation of Christ than his peers and an expectation for the promised reward of redemption that comes through faith. He is also a man with a mysterious, compelling, germinating calling from God that not even he totally understood.

In summary, according to Paul, Moses is a righteous man of faith, operating from the heart of God for the deliverance of a people with whom he deeply identifies; and so he goes out to "*look on their hard labors*" (Exodus 2:11). God always calls His children to minister to people. As westerners we tend to think in terms of vocations and ministries and income, but God thinks in terms of people. If your goal is just to become a doctor or a teacher or an artist or a mechanic or a maid or a pastor and you're not envisioning the people group God is sending you to through that vocation, you're missing God's highest in and through you. It's not just about status and titles and pay day! Who are the people God is asking you to minister to with His love?

I can imagine Moses praying and wondering what could possibly be done to change the plight of the Hebrew slaves, the people group he felt drawn to. Then he happens upon an Egyptian beating one of the Hebrew slaves, according to Exodus 2:11.

The cruelty and unfairness demonstrated by the Egyptian moves this compassionate, righteous man of faith into action to defend the defenseless slave. He must stand up against cruelty and unfairness and unjust behavior. His mysterious, compelling calling to redeem God's people from suffering stands up inside of him. So, after checking his surroundings to make sure no one was looking, he intervenes and ends up killing the Egyptian and hiding his body in the sand.

Moses is confronted with one nation oppressing and hating another nation.

"And he saw an Egyptian beating a Hebrew . . . So he looked this way and that, and when he saw there was no one around, he struck down the Egyptian and hid him in the sand." –Exodus 2:11

We've already established that the Pharaoh felt threatened by the Hebrews because there were so many of them. He was afraid that they would become a mightier nation than the Egyptians and eventually overthrow Egyptian rule. We also read in Genesis 46:34 that shepherds were loathsome to the Egyptians, and Scripture tells us that the Hebrews were shepherds. So, here we have one nation oppressing another because of a leader's paranoia and a general bias amongst the Egyptian population, which probably made it very easy for the Pharaoh to implement his oppressive laws. Most of his followers would have felt that shepherds don't deserve respect; after all, they were loathsome. They would have agreed that law-enforced slavery is a good way of controlling them.

My first "ugly" encounter with one nation oppressing another in this way is still very vivid in my memory. I was about nine years old when I was awakened in the deep of the night by shouting and pounding and swearing coming from the maid's quarters in our back yard. My dog was the first one to fly out of my bed, barking ferociously. Next, my dad came storming down the passage dressed in just his shorts and a vest and I think something like a baseball bat in his hand. My mom and I trailed behind. Before we even got outside, we heard the maid's door being beaten off its hinges. The maid was screaming, men were screaming, dogs were barking, by this time we were outside screaming. What was going on?

Come to find out, the police were executing a raid. You see, by law, all Black people had to be out of White communities by nine o'clock every evening. The only Black people that were allowed to stay were the maids who lived in the maids' quarters of their White "bosses," and they had to be in their quarters until the following morning. Our maid was Black, and the police were doing a neighborhood raid to make sure that the maids did not have boyfriends or husbands or children in their quarters.

By law, a maid was not allowed to have anybody with her after nine at night. She was usually allowed to keep a baby with her until the baby was weaned, and then the baby had to be taken to grandparents or other family members who lived on the outskirts of town in Black communities.

The maid saw her children and family only when she was allowed to go home, possibly for a weekend once a month, sometimes more often depending on the generosity of her "boss" or "missus." Even though her family could visit her during the day, the "missus" or "boss" often did not allow this because she was expected to work from morning till night—at least, that's how it was in the neighborhood where I lived. Thankfully, there were generous "bosses" who actually did have compassion, but too many did not.

I stood at the entrance of our maid's quarters, horrified at what I was witnessing. White Afrikaner policemen were in her room screaming and swearing at her in Afrikaans, making sure she had no one with her, which she did not. She stood there, skimpily dressed in her night gown, screaming and crying, and no one had any regard or respect for her body or her privacy or her feelings. I heard them call her a "kaffirmeid" several times, which was an Afrikaans term for a Black woman similar to the term "Nigger woman" in America. This was a term White Afrikaners in our neighborhood often used to describe how loathsome Black maids were to them. They were letting her know that she deserved no respect and wasn't going to get any because she was Black or, as they put it, because she was a "kaffirmeid."

I had grown up with the term "kaffir" (Nigger) being used by White people in my neighborhood in a derogatory way when referring to Black people, but never before had I actually witnessed in such a graphic, real-life, shocking way the bias and hateful emotions that accompanied that word. What was even more shocking to me was that some of these White men were deacons in the Dutch Reformed Church down the street. On Sundays they sat in the deacon pews with their black suits and white ties and "I-love-Jesus" smiles on their faces. To witness the hatred and swear words and derogatory behavior towards our maid coming from these so-called church leaders left me speechless and confused.

After they finally left, my dad fixed the maid's door as best he could, and we all went back to bed with not so much as a single apology to her. Everybody was numb and speechless, and I remember my dad being extremely angry and irate. I couldn't figure out whether his anger was based on the inconvenience of being woken up and having to fix a broken door knowing he had to get up very early to go to work the next morning, or whether he was angry because of the police's terrible, violent behavior. Looking back, I suppose it was a bit of both. At the time, I was too scared and shocked to ask. However, as my parents went back into their bedroom, I heard my dad mention to my mom that some of the policemen present were deacons in the Dutch Reformed Church down the street. He, too, even though he didn't attend church, was struck by the hypocrisy of the men's behavior. Nobody got much sleep the rest of the night.

The next morning, while I was having breakfast in the kitchen, our maid walked in to start her day. My parents had already left for work. As she looked at me, her eyes reflected such an acute mixture of pain, resignation and deep sorrow—and maybe even hatred—that it made me feel extremely uncomfortable. I got up and left for the bus stop. I wanted to apologize, but I didn't know what to say. Throughout my life, I was told by teachers, pastors, friends, parents—pretty much everybody in my world—that Black people had no rights, and that by law they had to be kept in their place, which was a place of submission and servant hood to White people. Do you recognize a pharaoh and slavery mindset?

And yet, as I looked into her eyes that morning, simultaneously remembering the events of the previous night and recollecting the faces of churchgoing so-called Jesus-loving policemen abusing her, none of that made sense anymore. I walked to the bus stop wondering what I was going to say to her when I got home from school because, in actual fact, she was a friend. Actually, she was, for all practical purposes, a nanny. She's the one I came home to while my parents were still at work. She's the one that made my bed, ironed my clothes, polished my shoes, listened to my chatter when I got home, and addressed and solved just about every household need I had.

The quality of her work quickly declined after this event, and soon afterwards my parents fired her and employed a new maid. I'm sad to admit that I don't remember her name anymore, but I still have a vivid memory of her standing in the doorway of the kitchen with those eyes . . .

As I've already mentioned, during my childhood there were eleven official nationalities in South Africa, two White and nine Black, and just about every nationality had a problem with the other—nation against nation, Black against Black, White against White, Black against White, White against Black—the only difference being that the two White nationalities could oppress the nine Black nationalities and get away with it by law.

Pharaoh mindsets and slavery mindsets were rife amongst all the nationalities, Black and White, and these mindsets were slowly eroding the very fiber of God's blessing on South Africa. What God did at the Battle of Blood River was not for the exaltation of one nation; it was for the redemption of everybody. It was a testimony of His existence and a call to follow Him and glorify Him and His kingdom by executing His calling to make God disciples of all nations.

I did not know it at the time of this incident, but there was a calling growing in my heart, accompanied by a Christ-like sense of righteousness. Many years later, as a Dutch Reformed Minister, I would be forced to make hard choices based on Black and White animosity; especially White Afrikaner animosity towards Blacks within the framework of the Dutch Reformed Church.

Moses, too, did not fully grasp his calling yet, but he already had a Christ-like sense of righteousness so that when he was confronted with a choice in that moment of seeing the Egyptian abusing a Hebrew slave, he followed his heart which, according to Paul, was the heart of God. He intervened and most likely saved the slave's life by killing an abusive oppressor and jeopardizing his own life and future in the process.

Moses is confronted with brothers fighting brothers.

"He went out the next day, and behold, two Hebrews were fighting with each other; and he said to the offender, 'Why are you striking your companion?' But he said, 'Who made you a prince or a judge over us? Are you intending to kill me as you killed the Egyptian?'" – Exodus 2:13-14

While still at university and working full time as a teller, I rented a quaint, old-fashioned little house close to the university and got a roommate to help with the rent. The roommate was the son of friends of my parents. My parents knew their friends very well, but did not know the son at all; they just assumed he was as nice and decent as his parents. It turned out that he was young and irresponsible and an alcoholic who came home late and drunk after work most nights. Needless to say, the arrangement didn't work, which left me in a predicament, because I couldn't afford the rent on my own. So, I had to move out.

A lot was happening in my life at the time: exams and tension, work and tension, not being able to keep up with the rent, alcoholic roommate and tension, having to find another place to live, the logistics of moving, did I mention tension? Stress! Then I had adults, including my parents on the side, criticizing me, because I shouldn't have rented the house in the first place; and they were right. I just loved the little house with its wooden floors and tub with feet and brass fixtures and front porch, so I followed my emotions instead of good sense, thinking that having a roommate couldn't be so bad.

The day I had to move, I borrowed a trailer and hitched it onto the back of my dad's truck. When I arrived at the house, I was unable to back the trailer into the driveway, having never done it before. No matter how hard I tried, I just couldn't get the hang of it. My neighbor had apparently been watching and finally came over and suggested I unhitch the trailer and push it into the driveway by hand, and he offered to help me do it.

At that moment, all the tension and stress of several months erupted, and I rudely told him that I didn't need anybody's help, and that I was doing quite fine, and that I wished other adults would just leave me alone. He was taken by such surprise that he took off back to his house and left me standing there with terrible remorse, but not enough to go after him and apologize. I was stubborn and proud and mad; however, it took me but a minute to realize that he was right, and so I sheepishly unhitched the trailer and pushed it into the driveway.

I was so upset with the world and with life and so bound up in a slavery mindset of my own, that I refused to accept help from a very well-meaning, good-hearted neighbor. I brushed him off like a piece of dirt and stomped on him. Really, I used him as a punching bag, releasing all my frustration and hurt on him, and all he was doing was trying to help. And to make things worse, I was a deacon in the church that he attended. Did I mention something about hypocrisy earlier in this chapter? Today, I wish I had gone after him and at least apologized for my bad behavior!

It's pretty obvious the slaves knew that Moses was one of them. Having him walk amongst them dressed like an Egyptian prince acting like he cared about them while living off the fat of the land in the midst of their suffering and abuse just irked the living daylights out of them. *Who made you a prince or judge over us*" (Exodus 2:14).

"Who exactly are you, Moses? Are you Egyptian, or are you Hebrew? You dress and act like an Egyptian, and yet you spend most of your days amongst us slaves. And now you've killed an Egyptian soldier supposedly for the sake of one of us. Who do you think you are? Go away; we don't need you, and we don't want you."

Moses was trying to help just like my neighbor was trying to help me, but the Hebrew slaves were so oppressed and angry at the world and hurting so badly that they threw his help back in his face. They couldn't discern the real deal, because their lives were muddied with trauma and pain and distrust and a slavery mindset (Exodus 2:14). The Pharaoh was keeping them in physical slavery, but a slavery mindset was keeping them in emotional, mental and spiritual slavery, blinding them to the possibility of redemption, especially coming from the likes of Moses.

"What are you, Reverend? Are you an Afrikaner or are you a 'kaffer-boetie' (lover of Niggers)?" This was the gist of many confrontations I had with several Dutch Reformed Church leaders and members after becoming a pastor. Apartheid or racial segregation had been abolished by this time, but it was still living in the hearts of people. Some were right in my face about it, crude and straightforward, while others were much subtler and politically correct about it; but all were antagonistic and made sure I understood their point of view.

They wanted me to understand that even though the law had changed, the boundaries had not. There was the White part of town with the White Dutch Reformed Church, and the Black part of town with the Black Dutch Reformed Church, and the Colored part of town (not to be confused with the term "Colored" as used in America). In South Africa, if a Black person and White person had children together, their offspring were considered Colored or Brown and they formed a third, separate people group with a third, separate Dutch Reformed Church. The Colored (Brown) people and Black people were not allowed to attend the White Dutch Reformed Church, because they weren't White; actually, to be more exact, they weren't White Afrikaners.

You see, not only did many members of the White Dutch Reformed Church have a problem with Blacks and Coloreds; they also had a problem with White English-speaking people. Before South Africa gained its independence from England in 1910 by becoming a Republic, the Boers, who later became known as Afrikaners, had to fight two bloody wars against the British. During this time, thousands of Boer wives and children died horrible deaths in concentration camps set up by the British, and many Boers felt hatred and bitterness towards the British as a result. Many of my congregation members still harbored hatred for the English and anybody who spoke English, which included me.

Yes, just to complicate matters, my grandfather, after he had returned from fighting in the Second World War, decided to change the household language to English. Everybody else in his family spoke Afrikaans. He put his son, my dad, into an English school and refused to speak Afrikaans to my grandmother who couldn't speak a word of English at the time. If only I could have been a fly on the wall to witness their interaction. He believed that English would become the "world language," and if you wanted to achieve great heights in this world, you needed to master the language.

My mom's family is also Afrikaans, but her mother married an English man when my mom was very young, prompting their home language to become English too. While I was growing up, when we went to family reunions, everybody spoke Afrikaans except us. It was quite humorous actually. Several of my congregation members failed to see the humor though. Here I was, a minister in the Dutch Reformed Church for White Afrikaners, irritating many because I openly spoke English to my parents and Afrikaans to my congregation members and on top of that, I refused to implement segregation in the local White Dutch Reformed congregation.

I refused to walk up to Black or Colored people visiting our service on a Sunday morning and ask them to leave because they weren't White Afrikaners. I also refused to turn a blind eye if a Black or Colored person needed help when I knew our congregation was in a position to help. In my mind, I would be denying Christ if I did that. *Therefore from now on we recognize no one according to the flesh . . . Therefore if anyone is in Christ, he is a new creature*" (2 Corinthians 5:17). *"We are ambassadors for Christ"* (2 Corinthians 5:20).

By this time in my life, I had had two very real, tangible encounters with Jesus Christ, and nothing would cause me to deny my Friend. I was an ambassador for Christ only! Soon a formal case was made against me with the Church Circuit in the form of what was known as an article 12, which stated that I could not constructively lead the congregation because I had become a figure of dissention. Some members of my congregation, including several deacons and elders, wanted the Dutch Reformed pastors of the Circuit to give them the legal authority to fire me. Therefore, the Circuit was compelled to launch an investigation into my conduct as a pastor and leader of my congregation. Anger and animosity towards me was escalating.

The wrath of Pharaoh

"When Pharaoh heard of this matter, he tried to kill Moses. But Moses fled from the presence of Pharaoh and settled in the land of Midian." – Exodus 2:15

Moses had killed an Egyptian soldier. In the eyes of Pharaoh, he was clearly an activist for Hebrew slaves, a traitor that could no longer be tolerated. The gist was, "Moses cannot be trusted. Put a bounty on his head and get rid of him!"

Once again the edict of Pharaoh that had threatened to take his life when he was a baby was pursuing him, and this time there was no one in Egypt who could intervene, not even the princess. If he wanted to stay alive, he had to leave the country. His hope of helping the slaves was dashed against the wrath of Pharaoh and the rejection of his fellow brethren.

Two years after I was ordained as a minister in the Dutch Reformed Church, three years after ministering in my first Dutch Reformed Congregation, I resigned and left the Dutch Reformed Church. I did this after an intense confrontation with outspoken Afrikaner Nationalists and the inaction of a "silent majority" who were too afraid to take a stand. I had also endured interactions with many pastors who felt their job security was more important than upholding the principles of Christ and I was forced to watch faithful ones suffer terribly under the merciless persecution from fellow brothers and sisters.

Eventually, I was forced to leave South Africa to resettle in what was a foreign country to me at the time, the United States of America, because I could not find work in South Africa. No church that served Afrikaners, wanted me because I was considered a controversial figure in those circles and other churches didn't want me because I wasn't trained in their doctrine. Additionally, the secular workplace didn't want me because I was White; the government was bent on enforcing affirmative action to right the wrongs of apartheid. If I was going to survive, I had to leave South Africa.

Moses didn't just leave; he had to flee at a moment's notice, leaving behind everybody and everything that was precious to him, to carve out a new existence and, dare I say, a new identity or calling in a foreign country called Midian? Did he miss God? What was it that rose up in him every time he went out to watch the Hebrew slaves? Was he wrong in standing up for them? Who was he anyway, and what made him think that he had a calling to help the slaves? I'm sure he was still mulling over these questions in his mind when God visited him forty years later, commissioning him to go back and finish what he had started. *"Who am I, that I should go to Pharaoh, and that I should bring the sons of Israel out of Egypt?"* says Moses to God forty years later in Exodus 3:11.

Most mainstream theologians choose to accuse Moses of being overzealous when he attacked the Egyptian in an attempt to save a slave. They say he acted ahead of God's timing and therefore ended up in the predicament of exile punishment. These are assumptions that theologians make because it looks like his calling and action to bring redemption to the Hebrews don't match the actual result which put him in exile for forty years while the Hebrew slavery continued.

Surely, if God were in it, Moses would not have ended up in exile for forty years in a foreign country called Midian. Would God really call a person to action and then allow circumstances to make that calling look paradoxical by a result that absolutely contradicts the calling? No, say mainstream theologians, he must have been overzealous. His zeal got him into trouble.

The only problem I have with these accusations and explanations is that Paul distinctly tells us in Hebrews 11:24-26 that faith was Moses' motivation, not zeal. Paul commends Moses for his faith and the fact that he wasn't afraid to uphold the righteousness of Christ while knowing that it could jeopardize his life. *"Considering the reproach of Christ greater riches than the treasures of Egypt; for he was looking to the reward"* (Hebrews 11:24-26).

I believe Moses was right on track. God was honing Moses into the phenomenal leader he had to become in order to lead a broken nation out of slavery—not just physical slavery, but mental, emotional and spiritual slavery. Moses had to pass some stringent tests to make the grade, whilst being molded by God into the man of God that he needed to become. Not only would he have to endure the rejection of his brethren, the wrath of Pharaoh, the loss of his family and friends and country, a life of exile as a stranger in a foreign land, but even an attempt by God Himself to kill him on the way back to Egypt (Exodus 4:24).

At the time of his exile, I'm sure Moses was totally unaware of the heavenly dynamics at work in his life. His reality was sitting at a well in Midian, alone, probably dazed, wondering where he was supposed to go next (Exodus 2:15). The truth is, his exile was just the beginning, but it was a good beginning. Moses had passed the test. He stayed true to the righteousness of Christ in the midst of Pharaoh's wrath and his brethren's rejection.

The next test would be the silence of God for forty years. Would he still love God and honor His calling after forty years of apparent desertion by God? *"Eli, Eli, Lama sabachthani? My God, My God, why have you forsaken me?"* (Matthew 27:46)

I sat in my prayer closet after resigning the Dutch Reformed Church, and all I could utter was, "I have nothing to say." Then I would sit there in God's silence and eventually just sob until I couldn't sob any longer. This went on for months and months. Why did I spend nine long, hard years of my life studying to be a Dutch Reformed minister, wait another year before being commissioned by a congregation, then go through almost another year of scrutiny to become their pastor, only to see it go up in smoke within two short, stormy years? I had invested roughly thirteen years of my life . . . and to what end? Silence! "My God, my God, why have you forsaken me?"

Are you living an apparent paradox? Are you drowning in God's silence? Are you experiencing the terror and agony of thinking that you've done something that has caused God to turn His back on you? If that is you, I want to admonish you out of Joshua 1:9, *"Be strong and courageous! Do not tremble or be dismayed, for the Lord your God is with you wherever you go."* You are not forsaken by God!

If it is any consolation to you, it took years and years of God sloughing layers and layers of pharaoh mindsets and slavery mindsets off of me before a Scripture like Romans 8 finally travelled from my head to my heart and I actually could let go of my spiritual "Egypt" and embrace the new spiritual "Midian" in which I found myself. Only then did I enter a new day with God.

So, my advice to you is to let go of your Egypt and embrace your Midian. The sooner you do, the sooner God can get on with your training and turn your paradox into the real deal.

"For I am persuaded, that neither death, nor life, nor angels, nor principalities, nor things present, nor things to come, nor powers, nor height, nor depth, nor any other creature, shall be able to separate us from the love of God, which is in Christ Jesus our Lord" – Romans 8:38-39

CHAPTER 4

Midian A.k.a. The Silence of God

I sit, and I wait . . .
I pray, and I wait . . .
I read and study and assimilate, and I wait . . .
I praise and worship Him, and I wait . . .
I go about my daily business, and I wait . . .
I decree and believe and plan and strategize and work, and I wait . . .
I sit, I pray, I read, I study, I assimilate, I praise, I
worship, I decree, I believe, I plan, I strategize,
I work . . .
I wait.

"Where are you, God?"

Was God M.I.A?

I was alone in a foreign land with no friends, no family, no support structure and seemingly . . . no God. Of course I knew, based on my theological training, that God wasn't really M.I.A., but that made little difference to the way I felt. I didn't just feel that God had deserted me; I felt like God's silence was evidence that He had rejected me. I was sure that He was disappointed in me. I had let Him down. I couldn't fulfill my assignment. I couldn't lead people to lay down their differences and love Jesus and live from the heart of Christ. I failed my Friend, and now He had turned His back on me, leaving me to wallow in my failure.

Seemingly my punishment was abandonment by the One that meant the most to me, and I was convinced that I deserved nothing less than His abandonment. After all, I was a hopeless failure!

I beat myself up like this for years after I resigned the Dutch Reformed Church, and for years it seemed to me that God remained silent, remained M.I.A., just confirming what I thought . . . I had been rejected by Him. And yet, I still pursued Him, cried out to Him, longed for Him, ached for Him, missed Him, looked for signs of Him everywhere. It took years for me to realize that He was not mad at me—that, in fact, He was right there transforming and healing my heart!

Divine boot camp of faith

"But Moses fled from the presence of Pharaoh and settled in the land of Midian, and he sat down by a well. Now the priest of Midian had seven daughters; and they came to draw water and filled the troughs to water their father's flock. Then the shepherds came and drove them away, but Moses stood up and helped them and watered their flock. When they came to Reuel their father, he said, 'Why have you come back so soon today?' So they said, 'An Egyptian delivered us from the hand of the shepherds, and what is more, he even drew the

*water for us and watered the flock.' He said to his daughters, 'Where
is he then? Why is it that you have left the man behind? Invite him to
have something to eat.' Moses was willing to dwell with the man."* –
Exodus 2:15-21

Moses had to walk through a foreign, arid desert country, and so it's only
logical that he would remain on the trails that led to water. His survival
in the desert depended on his ability to find water, and it is this need for
water that eventually led him to a specific well, which led him to the next
chapter of his life.

Moses' need for water was my need for an income. The only other skill
I had besides pastoring a church was working with American Saddlebred
horses, and so I was lured to America by work as a groom on an American
Saddlebred horse farm; and this too would lead to the next chapter of my
life.

Once a pastor, always a pastor
*"And He gave some as . . . pastors . . . for the equipping of the saints
for the work of service"* - Ephesians 4:11,12.

When you have a pastor's heart, you are filled with compassion for anything or anyone who is suffering. A pastor's heart intuitively wants to help.
Many people today serve others with pastors' hearts, though they don't
always necessarily officially carry the title of pastor. It's a gift . . . no, let
me rephrase that. According to Paul, they who carry the pastor anointing
are themselves gifts to mankind . . . especially to and from the church of
Jesus Christ (Ephesians 4:11, 12).

By God's grace, He gives certain people the gift of compassion or
pastorship, and then He gifts those same people to their environment
as agents of love and compassion. Wherever people with pastors' hearts
find themselves, they have this compulsion to fix things that are broken,
to intervene where an injustice is being practiced, to heal, to set free, to

serve, to love. They often have a history of brokenness themselves, giving them immense understanding and empathy for others who are suffering.

Try picturing Moses sitting at the well, probably tired and a little forlorn, wondering what to do with the rest of his life. As far as we know, he had never been outside the borders of Egypt and, if he had, I think it's safe to assume it was just for a short time and probably with a royal entourage. After all, he was royalty.

This was a different journey. Moses was relocating, alone, without a plan or a destination, fleeing from a tyrant who wanted to kill him. The well is the first point where he apparently felt safe enough, far away enough from Pharaoh, to actually linger and rest and maybe lick his wounds a little. He definitely had wounds. Besides the fact that he had to process the loss of family, stature, country, friends and so much more, he also had to process the rejection of the Hebrew slaves, which possibly implied the rejection of his calling. Stephen tells us in Acts 7:25, *"And he [Moses] supposed that his brethren understood that God was granting them deliverance through him, but they did not understand."* I'm sure Moses was mulling over the question, "Why did they not understand?"

I don't profess to know exactly what was going on in the mind of Moses as he sat by the well, but what happened next is just another testimony of his calling. He had a pastor's heart and so, when he saw a group of male shepherds bullying a group of female shepherds who were trying to water their father's flock, he intervened. True to the anointing resting upon him, he jumped into action, just like he had done with the slave back home, chasing the men away and helping the women water their sheep.

I'm sure he looked like a shining Egyptian knight in armor, coming to the aid of damsels in distress. Yes, Moses was so immersed in the Egyptian culture that he absolutely looked like an Egyptian . . . which is why the women, when they returned home with their flock, told their father that an Egyptian had helped them (Exodus 2:19).

Jethro, a priest with a pastors' heart, was appalled that his daughters had not invited the stranger home for dinner. They were so glad to get the flock watered and home without having to deal with the mean shepherds that they had forgotten their manners. So, at their father's command, they rushed back to the well and brought Moses home for dinner, and the rest is history. Moses stayed at Jethro's invitation, married one of Jethro's daughters, had children and started shepherding Jethro's flock (Exodus 2:21-22; 3:1).

All of this began at a well for Moses. My "well" was a horse farm in America, and I was slowly but surely becoming acquainted with my environment on the farm and with the other grooms and their lives. They were students working part-time to supplement their incomes and to add American Saddlery to their resumes. None of them knew the Lord. Some were into wild parties and the predicaments that these parties often presented, some were dealing with relationship problems, others with the aftermath of rape, drugs, booze, etc. So, as time went by, I became immersed in their worlds and wants and needs. Once a pastor, always a pastor . . .

Horse manure and a zoom lens

"Every branch in Me that does not bear fruit, He takes away; and every branch that bears fruit, He prunes it so that it may bear more fruit." – John 15:2

Moses landed at a well in a foreign country called Midian; I landed at an American Saddlebred horse farm in a foreign country called America. And even though I don't really know what Moses was thinking while he sat at that well, I do know what I was thinking one morning while I was shoveling horse manure out of one of the stables. It was hot! I was sticky with perspiration and oh so miserable, lonely and tired. My thoughts were a hurricane of memories of the congregation I had left behind and the whole resignation scenario. I pictured smug pastors and elders and deacons and others standing in the hallway of the stables laughing at my humiliation as I shoveled horse manure, while they were still enjoying the pleasures of their positions and lives. The tears were streaming down my face, and it was all I could do to control myself so that the other grooms didn't hear me cry.

It was at that moment that I suddenly became vividly aware of my pride and offense and unforgiveness. It was as though my being became a zoom lens that zoomed in on my heart, and what I saw was ugly—a lot uglier than the smug faces I had imagined just moments ago. I literally saw how my sense of humiliation was actually pride in disguise. After all, many people shoveled horse manure as an honest living. What was so humiliating about that? I also saw the picture of the people laughing at me as an illustration of my own offense and unforgiveness towards those that I had left behind.

I broke down and cried some more, but this time it was tears of repentance. Oh, I couldn't bear the thought of disappointing my Lord and Friend even more than I already had by harboring offence and pride and unforgiveness. Through the tears I prayed, "God, please help me. Please! Help me!" I was physically, mentally and spiritually exhausted!

As I've already indicated, God was sloughing off layers and layers of my own pharaoh and slavery mindsets, and this was just the beginning. God was also testing my resolve to follow Him no matter what, even if He was seemingly M.I.A. Was I set up by God to live what I preached? Would I live up to the standards that God called people to live up to through my sermons? Would I put my life where my words and His words were? Could I sacrifice my all and trust Him to sustain and establish me in spite of all the losses and rejections and pain and failures and fears?

Could I live and believe and demonstrate 1 Peter 5:10 which states, *"After you have suffered for a little while, the God of all grace, who called you to His eternal glory in Christ, will Himself perfect, confirm, strengthen and establish you"*?

Could I live and believe and demonstrate the one sermon that I preached over and over to the congregation I left behind from John 12:24–26: *"Truly, truly I say to you, unless a grain of wheat falls into the earth and dies, it remains alone; but if it dies, it bears much fruit. He who loves his life loses it, and he who hates his life in this world will keep it to life eternal. If anyone serves Me, he must follow Me; and where I am, there My servant will be also; if anyone serves Me, the Father will honor him"*?

Could I die? Could I die and still believe and trust God? I had once pleaded with a congregation to let go of their pride, heritage, unforgiveness, offence, fears and everything that was seemingly precious to them. I asked them to die to themselves and to their so-called Afrikanership and serve Jesus and His agenda, trusting Him to protect them and establish them and nurture what was precious to them, even their Afrikanership. All but a handful had refused, and now the question was, what say I? Could I myself say yes to that sermon?

Make no mistake, I was dying, and looking back, without trying to pretend that I had the level of purity that Moses had, I believe I lived a "yes" and still am. I lived a "yes," albeit in a clumsy and sometimes carnal way, often tripping over myself and others. But, by God's grace, I passed and am passing the test—with difficulty, but passing. By no means do I profess that I have arrived yet, but I'm beginning to understand what Paul meant when he wrote 2 Timothy 4:7, *"I have fought the good fight, I have finished my course, I have kept the faith: in the future is laid up for me the crown of righteousness."* Paul was referring to the crown of righteousness he was expecting as a reward for keeping the faith when he arrived in heaven, and boy, do I look forward to that one. However, I've already noted that there is also a crown of righteousness, a reward, on this earth, in this lifetime. It is the blessing I wrote about in the introduction to this book. It is the life of John 15, abiding in Christ and Christ in us, asking whatever you want and it being given to you, the life I'm aspiring to. I've also noted that the journey there is not for the fainthearted.

At that moment in that stable, I was not thinking about John 15 or a blessing column in an introduction to my book or a reward. I was thinking about exhaustion and what a failure I was and the fact that God's silence or absence was as good as His judgment finger pointing at me. Adding pride and offence and unforgiveness was just more fuel, I thought, for His judgment on me.

The fact that there is no condemnation in Christ Jesus according to Romans 8:1 didn't even feature anywhere in my thoughts. And if I had stopped to think about it, where did the zoom lens come from, exposing the state of my heart to me? Today I know that God was there, pruning away (John 15:2). At the time, I was just too drenched in my sorrow to notice. However, I was not about to give up on God either.

I was bent on pursuing Him or dying trying . . . and little did I know that God intended for me to die, at least the part of me that wasn't suitable for a John 15 lifestyle. Little did I know or understand at the time that God's silence was an open invitation to pursue Him to deeper places, places I had never been before in Him. I learned that God's silence is like deep calling to deep (Psalm 42:7).

God was pruning me ever so severely and every branch, every pharaoh and slavery mindset that was cut off, left an excruciating wound that tested my resolve to continue loving and trusting Him no matter what. But by God's grace, through the power and mercy of His Holy Spirit, I refused to let go of Him. I would live for Him, and I would die for Him. Many times on this journey, I thought I was dying for Him when, in reality, I was learning how to live for Him and more importantly, from Him.

Déjà vu

"Moses was willing to dwell with the man [Jethro], and he [Jethro] gave his daughter Zipporah to Moses." – Exodus 2:21.

I'm sure Moses felt relieved when Jethro invited him to stay. He had no idea where to go, so this place was as good as any. Jethro seemed hospitable and friendly and, quite possibly, Zipporah was pretty too. Why not stay and start a new life with a new family?

This seemed like a logical conclusion to me too when I met a pastor and his wife and they invited me to become their youth pastor and launch a youth ministry for troubled teenagers, something he had been dreaming about for a long time. They also invited me to live with them. Just like Moses, I accepted, and so began the next chapter of my life.

It wasn't long though before I found myself dealing with the same prejudices that confronted me in South Africa, only this time the prejudice was against troubled teenagers, not Black people. Different faces, different scenario, same mindsets, same outcome.

The congregation members eventually delivered an ultimatum to the pastor: he could choose between the teenage ministry which included me or them. Then followed the old, old story of people threatening to withdraw their financial support and leave the church if the youth ministry wasn't dissolved immediately.

The youth ministry was growing fast, and the members of the church felt threatened by the sheer numbers of teenagers coming to church. Even though I fully trained the congregation in how these teenagers would possibly act and especially how they would be dressed, their mode of dress and lifestyle still shocked congregation members, and some wanted out. Conflict started arising and growing as more and more adults convinced each other that the youth ministry wasn't for them, and that I wasn't for them, partly because I headed the youth ministry, and partly because some harbored a prejudice against women in the ministry and others against foreigners. Three strikes!

James wasn't kidding when he wrote about the destructive power of the tongue in James 3. Conflict also arose between the pastor and me as he was being torn between the congregation and the youth ministry, which, by the way, had been *his* dream. Ultimately, the teenagers actually behaved much better than us, the so-called adults.

I came to church one Sunday morning and was dismissed by the church board with a month's pay and a threat that if I questioned the decision at all, I would lose even the month's pay they were giving me. As far as they were concerned, I could go back to Africa where I belonged, because the youth ministry and I had caused nothing but heartache for them. At this point, the pastor had backed down completely, leaving me holding the hot potato. He chose to deny the fact that this particular youth ministry model targeting problem youth was his dream, launched at his initiative, and had been managed and overseen by him.

Leading up to this Sunday, I had tried my level best to get the youth ministry under an independent youth ministry that was already established in the surrounding area. I was also looking for other accommodations and bracing myself for the worst as relationships deteriorated. Their Sunday dismissal, therefore, did not come as a complete surprise, but the severe and ugly manner in which it transpired was shocking to me. It felt like déjà vu. Once again I found myself crowded out by pharaoh and slavery mindsets of church people, people who professed to love Jesus but chose to be governed by their worldly mindsets and fears instead of an unconditional love for Jesus and His kingdom. I also have to admit, as relationships deteriorated, sometimes their behavior brought out the worst of me, which I'm not proud of and which accentuated my own pharaoh and slavery mindsets that still had to be dealt with.

The truth is, the rejection from this congregation after experiencing the rejection in South Africa pierced so deeply that it almost totally devastated my faith in love. In the past, in South Africa, people had told me that I was naive to think that mankind could love the way Jesus did. I was starting to think maybe they were right. Sorrow is truly painful! I understood exactly what Jesus meant when he told Jerusalem in Luke 13:34, *"O Jerusalem, Jerusalem, the city that kills the prophets and stones those sent to her! How often I wanted to gather your children together, just as a hen gathers her brood under her wings, and you would not have it!"* According to Stephen in Acts 7:25, Moses also understood this level of sorrow. I was learning, just like Jesus and Moses did, that just because I had a calling, it did not mean that the people to whom God sent me were ready to receive what my calling entailed. I spent the next several years trying to make sense of that.

I was also learning about the existence of a spirit of intimidation and manipulation, which is a spirit of witchcraft that will do everything possible to prevent people and me from entering the promised land of John 15. Paul had it right when he wrote in Ephesians 6:12, *"For our struggle is not against flesh and blood, but against the rulers, against the powers, against the world forces of this darkness, against the spiritual forces of wickedness in the heavenly places."* I would actually have a few real encounters with this spirit several years later, making me realize just how real these dark forces are, but also letting me realize that I have the authority to resist them and make them flee in the name of Jesus.

Unconditional love really does exist

"Moses was willing to dwell with the man [Jethro]." – Exodus 2:21

Thank God for the Jethros of this world! No, not Leroy Jethro Gibbs from NCIS, but Jethro, the priest from Midian who gave Moses a safe haven to settle into. Doris was such a Jethro for me. She was a great-grandmother in her late seventies who stepped into my life as a stranger from a different city and gave me hope—actually, she saved my life.

As things were deteriorating in the congregation where I was a youth pastor, some "Jethro" congregation members took pity on me and stood up for me and the youth ministry—people who did not allow the wagging tongues to sway them. These people had the courage to walk next to me and hold up my arms. I am very grateful to them, but even their brave faithfulness could not stop the wave of bias. Eventually they too had to submit.

One of the deacons' wives looked at me one day and said, "I'm curious to see whether you can actually live the kind of faith you preach about." She knew I was going to be literally thrown out and left to fend for myself. I spent most of my days praying profusely and decreeing Scriptures of outcome and deliverance, and in the midst of my prayers and cries and decrees entered an elderly great-grandmother with a pastor's heart, seemingly out of nowhere. Yes, God does answer prayer, and He does honor faith, and He's not M.I.A., although it still took quite a long time for me to admit that He wasn't M.I.A.

I was tempted to think that the unconditional love I read about and preached about was just words on paper, but I chose to keep on believing and keep on praying. I desperately needed help because I knew things were moving to a point of explosion, and I knew the outcome wasn't going to be good for me. By God's grace, I chose to keep on believing, and God sent Doris.

Doris hugged me with what I found out later was one of her famous anointed hugs and took me to her home for lunch, and the rest is quite remarkable. She and her husband, Elwood, invited me to stay. I accepted, and they bathed me in the unconditional love of the Lord, the kind that I had started thinking did not exist, the kind I preached about and longed for. Little did we know then just how significant our relationship would become, not just for me, but for them too.

As I bathed in their love and my heart slowly, very slowly, started healing, a very serious prayer that started out small in South Africa began evolving and growing; it still grows louder and louder in my heart each day, even now.

A cry slowly erupted from the pit of my anguished being, "Lord, show me Your Glory and teach me Your ways (Exodus 33:13, 18). I want to do the things that Jesus did and greater things (John 14:12). I want to heal the sick, cast out demons, raise the dead and cleanse the lepers (Matthew 10:8) and do those greater things that You promised. I'm tired of playing church, Lord, tired of an academic relationship with a Book, tired of church politics and hypocrisy. I want to represent Your righteousness and Your kingdom on this earth in this lifetime (Matthew 6:33). I want to be known as Your disciple. I want to occupy and live from that place of intimacy in Jesus where I can ask whatever I want and it be done, because we are one. I want to bear the fruit of Your kingdom (John 15). Please, Lord, give me a burning bush experience like You did Moses in Exodus 3:2. Give me an Acts 2 experience like You did Your disciples, and set me ablaze for Your kingdom in the name of Jesus! I don't mind suffering for Your cause, Lord, but in the midst of it, *please* deliver the goods. I don't want to be just a babble of words; I want to be a demonstration of Your great and wonderful works (1 Corinthians 2:4). Lord, baptize me with Your power and presence, and let me live from Your heart. Let me be about our Father's business. Amen."

I sit, and I wait . . .
I pray, and I wait . . .
I read and study and assimilate, and I wait . . .
I praise and worship Him, and I wait . . .
I go about my daily business, and I wait . . .
I decree and believe and plan and strategize and work, and I wait . . .
I sit, I pray, I read, I study, I assimilate, I praise, I
worship, I decree, I believe, I plan, I strategize,
I work . . .
I wait . . .

Isaiah 49:4 says, *"I have toiled in vain, I have spent my strength for nothing and vanity; yet surely the justice due to me is with the Lord, and my reward with my God."*

I will wait some more . . .

Isaiah 49:7 and 23 say, *"⁷Kings will see and arise, princes will also bow down, because of the Lord who is faithful, the Holy One of Israel who has chosen You. ²³Kings will be your guardians and their princesses your nurses. They will bow down to you with their faces to the earth and lick the dust of your feet; And you will know that I am the Lord."*

Some things are worth waiting for!

Isaiah 49:23 says, *"Those who hopefully wait for Me will not be put to shame."*

I wait . . . hopefully!

What kind of relationship do you have with God? Is it academic, or is it real? Can you trust God to come through for you? Can you keep the faith when reality (people, lack of finances, sickness, loss, etc.) seems bent on destroying you or a loved one? Would you be prepared to sacrifice everything—your livelihood, your family, your country, things and people precious to you, just like Moses did, because you serve Jesus first and man second and man is forcing you to choose? Be truthful. If circumstances were threatening to change everything you hold dear, would your actions be governed by your belief in what you think is going to happen, or would your actions be governed by your faith in Jesus Christ? If everything were crumbling around you and God seemed M.I.A, would you still trust Him? Would you be prepared to pursue Him until you find Him in the midst of those circumstances, or will you walk away and give up on Him and submit to the circumstances?

Christians all over the world today are being confronted with one or more of the above scenarios. Maybe you're being confronted with one or more yourself right now. If you are not, you have been or you will be; so let me ask you again, is your relationship with God, your trust in Him, academic or real?

"Not everyone who says to Me, 'Lord, Lord,' will enter the kingdom of heaven, but he who does the will of My Father who is in heaven will enter." – Matthew 7:21

"So then, my beloved . . . work out your salvation with fear and trembling." – Philippians 2:12

"He who loves his life loses it, and he who hates his life in this world will keep it to life eternal. If anyone serves Me, he must follow Me; and where I am, there My servant will be also; if anyone serves Me, the Father will honor him." – John 12:26

CHAPTER 5

God's Ways Are Not Our Ways

"In a favorable time I have answered You, and in a day of salvation I have helped You." – Isaiah 49:8

"Now it came about . . . that the king of Egypt died. And the sons of Israel sighed . . . and they cried out; and their cry for help because of their bondage rose up to God . . . and God remembered His covenant with Abraham, Isaac, and Jacob." – Exodus 2:23-24

"Now, behold, the cry of the sons of Israel has come to Me; furthermore, I have seen the oppression with which the Egyptians are oppressing them. Therefore, come now, and I will send you [Moses] to Pharaoh, so that you may bring My people, the sons of Israel, out of Egypt." – Exodus 3:9-10

"For I am aware of their sufferings." – Exodus 3:7

"Let's get some things straight, Lord. First You gave me a calling from birth, and I put my heart and soul into that calling, only to get my heart severely broken. You also allowed a tyrannical Pharaoh to put a bounty on my head, first at birth, which was averted by the princess, and then later again, causing me to flee, leaving behind everything I held dear. And then, just in case You haven't noticed, I spent the past forty years of my life tending sheep that aren't even my own in what initially seemed like my personal God-forsaken desert.

"I even named my first child Gershom as an expression of being left by You as *'a sojourner in a foreign land'* (Exodus 2:22). Did that tell You something about how I felt? Did You even care? My firstborn reminds me every day of the fact that I had another life. As a matter of fact, I'm still connected to that life in a way that prevents me from truly settling and owning my own piece of real estate in Midian.

"I don't mean to be ungrateful. Really, I'm very thankful for Jethro and Zipporah and my children and the fact that my father-in-law entrusted his sheep business to my management. You did well hooking me up with Jethro, although I'm not quite sure how, because you chose to do it silently without my input.

"Egypt! You did not do well there. You forsook me and the Hebrew slaves and abandoned me for forty years. *Where have You been?!* You can't just come waltzing into my life after forty years of silence and expect to pick up where we left off as if nothing happened. Don't we have some issues to settle first?"

Now that I've gotten that little rant off my chest for Moses' sake, let's get on with the story.

God has already figured the way of escape into the equation.

"No temptation has overtaken you but such as is common to man; and God is faithful, who will not allow you to be tempted beyond what you are able, but with the temptation will provide the way of escape also, so that you will be able to endure it." – 1 Corinthians 10:13

While thinking about the Hebrew slaves and their terrible suffering, as well as Moses' suffering and my own, I started thinking about suffering in general. Right now at the time of this writing, I have several friends going through hard circumstances, some caused by life-threatening illnesses, others by financial difficulties, others by strained relationships, and the list goes on.

We all at some point get impatient and upset when bad circumstances just don't seem to end or when things don't work out the way we desire, causing all kinds of disruptions and pain to our lives.

Paul, however, reminds us in 1 Corinthians 10:13 that nothing we go through is new. It is all *"common to man."* The escape route has already been designed and implemented by God, and He understands our limits. He knows exactly when to intervene and when not to. And according to John 15:7, we have Christ and our Sword, the Word, as guarantees of victory *if* we abide in Christ and His Word in us.

So, why do we get pushed to our limits and seemingly sometimes beyond our limits? After all, Moses had basically given up on his dream and carved out a brand-new life in a brand-new country with a brand-new family and, if you look at the case of the Hebrew slaves, adults and babies actually died before God finally decided to intervene. What's up with that?

God's children lack knowledge
"My people are destroyed for lack of knowledge." – Hosea 4:6

Suffering is big topic that can fill an entire book by itself. In this chapter, I'm going to highlight a few mile markers. One of the reasons for suffering is found in Hosea 4:6. According to Hosea, the church has not yet gained sufficient knowledge of God that would cause them to trust Him and apply their faith in such a way that the church as an individual and the church as a corporate body lives and becomes a demonstration of promises like John 15.

In spite of the fact that God's children profess to know Jesus and are on their way to heaven after life on earth, most are not living long lives of abundance and victory on this earth, because we don't really understand spiritual warfare and the tools of warfare and the promises that God has put at our disposal.

God will often not intervene in areas where we are already equipped to exercise our authority in Christ. In those areas, we are expected to partner with Holy Spirit and wield our Sword, the Word, in Jesus' name and advance with faith into victory; and if we don't, we can very well perish . . . not in the sense that we go to hell, but in that we become victims of destruction on earth, *"destroyed for lack of knowledge."*

We often also don't understand Love Himself because few really engage in an intimate relationship with Him and, therefore, in our ignorance, we have failed to learn to hear His voice. Without His Voice guiding us like a rudder through the waters of life, we find ourselves at the mercy of life's relentless waves and demonic winds.

All I have to say about this is, get into the Word, dear friend, and meditate on it day and night, and do what is written in it. Then, *"you will make your way prosperous, and then you will have success"* (Joshua 1:8). *"Faith [which leads to victory] comes from hearing [knowledge] and hearing [knowledge] by the word of Christ"* (Romans 10:17). Without knowledge of the living God, faith is hard to come by, and His voice is drowned out by external circumstances and voices.

If you don't spend time meditating on and chewing and digesting the Word and allowing Holy Spirit to ferment that Word in your heart on a daily basis, you will lack the faith that comes from knowledge when it matters most (Matthew 17:20)—when terminal disease attacks your body, when financial ruin knocks at your door, when divorce strips you of precious family, when the woes of life eat you for dinner.

Being a child of God, but lacking knowledge, means you'll be saved, but at the same time consumed by the fire of life (1 Corinthians 3:15). And the fire I'm referring to is not necessarily the one that kills the body and destroys material belongings and relationships; more importantly, it's the one that eats away at the heart of faith, hope and love. Good salt-of-the-earth folk who go to church and abide by the laws of the land and who profess Jesus as their Lord and Savior are suffering and slowly dying from impoverished hearts, because of a *"lack of knowledge"* of the living God.

I have only recently started appreciating the full meaning of Hosea 4:6 and Matthew 17:20 and John 15:7. The Bible, our Sword, through the power of Holy Spirit, can break down any and every stronghold; but you have to wield it in knowledge, by faith in Jesus. This means, dear friend, we have to take time out of our busy schedules every day to go aside and allow Holy Spirit to drench us in His Word. This includes reading it, meditating on it, imagining it, pondering it, chewing on it, digesting it, allowing it to ferment in our souls and spirits, savoring it, memorizing it, and writing down the insights that flow from our encounters with the Word through Holy Spirit until it launches us into a very intimate, personal, tangible relationship with the living God so that we actually start hearing His voice and His revelation for each day. Then and only then can we go out to practice and apply what we've learned. The Word launches us into the mind and heart of God where we meet Him in a very personal way. It's in that personal interaction that He transforms us so that we get to live from His heart and mind to our influence circle through His revelation.

I have found that as I have yielded myself to this process on a daily basis, a transformation has occurred in me. I am becoming a new person, *"who is being renewed to a true knowledge according to the image of the One who created"* me (Colossians 3:10), and that new person is much more apt to overcome and, even more important, to live victoriously.

"But we all, with unveiled face, beholding as in a mirror the glory of the Lord, are being transformed into the same image from glory to glory, just as from the Lord, the Spirit" (2 Corinthians 3:18). The mirror is God's nature, God's glory, looking back at us through the Word and through our personal encounters with Him; and every time we behold His face, His glory, we are transformed into His likeness. My only regret is that it's taken me so long to learn this truth.

A severe health crisis becomes my training ground for the above.

"Faith [which leads to victory] comes from hearing [knowledge] and hearing [knowledge] by the word of Christ" (Romans 10:17).

After I started living with Doris and Elwood, I once again found myself in the position of not earning an income. My work permit had to be adjusted, which meant that lawyers' fees and my regular bills began accumulating. I started maxing out my credit cards in an attempt to pay bills and the lawyer, and my anxiety levels were escalating. Eventually the stress hit a weak spot of mine, my colon. I have suffered from a spastic colon since childhood, and I had an acute attack during this time to the point that I was unable to straighten my body due to the pain. This went on for an entire year, with three-day attacks happening sometimes on a weekly basis.

I was still in my infant shoes as far as trusting the Lord and wielding my Sword was concerned, so I spent most of that year in anxiety instead of resting in the knowledge of God and faithfully wielding my Sword. Don't get me wrong, I was reading the Bible and praying and even decreeing the Word over my health and my finances and my life in general; but the anxiety in me was stronger than my faith in the Word and the Lord's deliverance. It took me that year and beyond to admit that I was living in anxious unbelief.

Towards the end of that year, Doris and Elwood and I travelled to Pennsylvania to attend an Apostle's Conference led by Randy Clark. I was in acute pain and really had to apply all the self-discipline I could muster in order to drive them to Pennsylvania and attend the conference.

In one of the evening services, Bishop Garlington preached about faith and wielding the Sword in faith. At one point in his sermon, he created so much faith in the room and in me that I put my hand on my stomach (which felt more like a rock than a stomach) and decreed the Scripture of the night over my colon and commanded it to be healed in the name of Jesus. Almost instantly, my stomach became soft and the pain went away;

by the next morning, the swelling had subsided, and the pain was gone. Praise God! Suddenly I understood the power of the Sword, and from that point on, I started exploring my newfound knowledge in God and faith.

I wish I could say everything changed in an instant, but it didn't. I still had a lot of anxiety, and I was still beating myself up because I continued to believe that I was a complete failure in the eyes of the Lord. However, this was a step forward and, slowly but surely, Holy Spirit started getting my attention on the matter. I had experienced the real, authentic Holy Spirit power of the Sword and faith in Jesus that night. That was the beginning of my journey to the truth of John 15:7. As you abide in Christ and the Word abides in you, Christ, through His Holy Spirit, releases powerful, transformational life from the Word into you and through you. I gradually started learning exactly what it meant to "abide in Christ" and to have "the Word abiding in me." Hopefully, by the end of this book, you will have too.

God's grace redeems suffering.

"And He has said to me, 'My grace is sufficient for you, for power is perfected in weakness. Most gladly, therefore, I will rather boast about my weaknesses, so that the power of Christ may dwell in me.'" – 2 Corinthians 12:9

"For the grace of God has appeared, bringing salvation for all men." – Titus 2:11

The author of suffering is the devil and the author of redemption is God and suffering is redeemed by the grace of God. Between the moment that we enter a time of suffering and the moment we finally reach our favorable time of salvation or deliverance that we read about in Isaiah 49:8, a period of grace is determined by God. During this grace period, God's children are pruned and refined into gold, provided they yield to God's pruning. During this same time, the people deceived by the enemy are offered the opportunity to witness the testimony of God's children as they faithfully endure trials and demonstrate God's great and wonderful works in and through their faith. These deceived individuals are given food for thought, a grace period to repent and change their ways.

This grace period is precious, as all parties involved are invited into a deeper richer experience with God; and those who accept the invitation grow from glory to glory in their understanding of how to live and demonstrate the kingdom of God on this earth (2 Corinthians 3:18). This grace period, however, is also dangerous as it often results in casualties on both sides—the side of God, and the side of the devil. Hence, we have the reality of suffering.

On God's side during this grace period, some people are called to martyrdom who actually give up their lives in faithfulness to Jesus as a testimony to those who take their lives; and, yes, not even babies are exempt from martyrdom. Don't forget, says Paul in Ephesians 6, our fight is ultimately against the *"schemes of the devil,"* and the devil has no conscience. Babies dying this very day of starvation in Africa, or being killed by a tyrannical Pharaoh in Exodus 1, or an insanely paranoid Herod in Matthew 2, or a twisted perverted individual somewhere in this modern world of ours are all part of the *"schemes of the devil"* to disgrace God's reputation in an attempt to get people to reject the one true living God.

For a set period of time, though, God by His grace allows martyrdom and persecution of His people and suffering in general so that somewhere in the crowd of onlookers a "Saul" or a "Sally" can observe, feel, think and analyze . . . who still needs time, or should I say still needs a period of grace to repent and enter into their day of salvation by comprehending and embracing Christ (Acts 7:58; 9:4).

The truth is, no amount of temporary suffering on this earth, no matter how horrific and traumatic, can match the suffering of eternal damnation and darkness that a lost soul enters into after death. If the horrific, cruel stoning of Stephen bought time for Saul to eventually meet Jesus on the road to Damascus and become Paul, then the way Stephen died had meaning. But even if it did not affect Saul who later became Paul, Saul would not have been able to plead ignorance about the truth of God at the day of judgment, because he saw and heard the dying testimony of Stephen.

Even babies crying because of starvation and thirst can bring people to the Lord and open their eyes to His salvation (Genesis 21:15-19). But even if their cries don't cause eyes to open, those cries will act as judgment when the perpetrators stand before God, because they weren't moved when they should have been. It is also important to note, those babies are not lost. Their souls go to heaven, as they have not reached the age of accountability yet. They go to heaven as martyrs.

Let's be clear though. It's not God's doing or His will for these things to happen; it's the devil's doing (Ephesians 6) and human lust and corruption (Genesis 3:6) that cause it. However, in spite of the devil's evil schemes and the actions caused by human lust and corruption, Romans 8:28 promises those who choose God, *"that God causes all things to work together for good to those who love God, to those who are called according to His purpose."* Romans 8:28 makes a very clear distinction between the children of God and the rest of mankind, provided the children of God are wielding their Swords, the Word, and exercising their faith or, as Romans 8:28 infers, provided they are loving God instead of cuddling their pharaoh and slavery mindsets.

The imposters amongst God's children, those who only want their ears tickled (2 Timothy 4:3) and those who are like whitewashed tombs just pretending (Matthew 23:27) are also flushed out and exposed during this time of grace, giving them opportunities to sober up and make better choices or suffer the consequences of their deceitful actions. This period of grace also produces great rewards for those who don't grow weary, who endure and make it to the day of deliverance with their faith still intact (Galatians 6:9). Joshua and Caleb are examples from our story of Moses and the Hebrew slaves, of people who made it to the day of deliverance and actually got to live the reward of their promised land (Joshua 1:3; 14:14).

On the enemy's side however, we find a group of people whose hatred and self-centered unbelief get cemented in by this grace period as they persist in their wicked ways, sending them to a destiny of darkness, to *"a furnace of fire [where] there will be weeping and gnashing of teeth [for eternity]"* (Matthew 13:50).

The redemption of Moses by the Egyptian princess and the midwives not carrying out the command of Pharaoh to kill Hebrew baby boys and the ten plagues are just a few examples of grace periods that were given to both Pharaohs in the story of Exodus at the cost of the Hebrew slaves' suffering, but instead of it bringing them to a day of deliverance, it brought them and Egypt to a day of utter destruction (Exodus 14:28). It also, however, sobered up a generation of Hebrew slaves living the consequences of rejecting the first offer of salvation by Moses and God, thus making them much more inclined to listen the second time around.

There is no excuse for evil.

"For since the creation of the world His invisible attributes, His eternal power and divine nature, have been clearly seen, being understood through what has been made, so that they are without excuse." – Romans 1:20

Scott Peck wrote an interesting book that describes evil and the people who choose it called *People of the Lie*[4]. I'm of the opinion that the two Pharaohs in the story of Exodus and Herod in Matthew's story of Jesus' birth, and even the story of someone like a modern-day Hitler, are just a few examples of people who would fit the description of Scott Peck's "people of the lie." All four of these leaders were given extended periods of grace to repent at the expense of others' suffering and dying, but they did not repent. Instead, they stubbornly chose evil.

It is because of God's grace though that, ultimately, when judgment day comes, nobody has an excuse when they stand before the Creator of this universe (Romans 1:20). The "people of the lie" and the "imposters"

---

[4] Scott Peck, People of The Lie (Touchstone Publisher, 1998)

and the "whitewashed tombs" and anybody else who rejected God will not be able to say they didn't know better. I personally would have had a hard time understanding Romans 1:20 if Jesus hadn't visited me as a teenager in my bedroom, offering me friendship and salvation. I know from personal experience now that Jesus, or should I say Grace Himself, will not allow people, even "people of the lie," to die in ignorance of who God is and the fact that we were created to live in communion with Him.

Every person, even that person living in the remotest part of the Amazon who has never met a Christian or the most hardened criminal with the hardest heart, will at some point during their lifetime, experience His grace and the revelation of who He is, according to Romans 1:20 and the verses that surround it. At some point during our existence on this earth, every person, after reaching the age of accountability, is confronted with the choice to either acknowledge Grace or reject Grace Himself; and Grace is often, but not always, represented through the living testimonies of God's children as they demonstrate real faith in real time while confronting real circumstances and demonstrating real victory, by the grace of God, through the power of Holy Spirit and in the name of Jesus Christ.

How are you living your life before God and before others? Are you a living sermon testifying about a living God, leading others into His heart and mind?

God is a covenant God:
He never forgets, and He does mercifully intervene.

"And God remembered his covenant with Abraham, Isaac and Jacob." – Exodus 2:24

"Can a woman forget her nursing child and have no compassion on the son of her womb? Even these may forget, but I will not forget you. Behold, I have inscribed you on the palms of My hands; your walls are continually before Me. Your builders hurry; your destroyers and devastators will depart from you." – Isaiah 49:15-17

In spite of a lack of knowledge and unbelief amongst God's children and the schemes of the devil and the lustful acts of mankind in general and the deception in which people live, God always preserves a remnant who remains faithful by His grace, who eventually get to taste the rewards of victory and salvation on this earth and become a testimony of His great goodness (1 Kings 19:18; Romans 9:28-29; Galatians 6:9).

God does intervene! If He didn't, nobody would make it to the finish line of faith.

God intervenes supernaturally.

"The angel of the LORD *appeared to him in a blazing fire from the midst of a bush; and he looked, and behold, the bush was burning with fire, yet the bush was not consumed . . . When the* LORD *saw that he turned aside to look, God called to him from the midst of the bush and said, 'Moses, Moses!' And he said, 'Here I am.'"* – Exodus 3:2, 4

"But Mary was standing outside the tomb weeping; and so, as she wept, she stooped and looked into the tomb; and she saw two angels in white sitting, one at the head and one at the feet, where the body of Jesus had been lying. And they said to her, 'Woman, why are you weeping?' She said to them, 'Because they have taken away my Lord, and I do not know where they have laid Him.' . . . she turned around and saw Jesus standing there . . . Jesus said to her, 'Mary!' She turned and said to Him in Hebrew, 'Rabboni!' [which means, Teacher]." – John 20:11-14

Moses had spent the past forty years sojourning. It seemed as though his calling was dead and God was M.I.A. Mary was convinced that Jesus was dead; she saw Him die on the cross. The one that she thought was the Messiah, the Redeemer of the Jews, was no longer in their midst. Moses had resigned himself to sojourning, and Mary had resigned herself to embalming Jesus' body and closing the chapter on His life. Great promises ended in heart-wrenching separation, and all they had left were memories mixed with sorrow until . . . God supernaturally intervened! One supernatural visitation reinstated their callings and set them on a path of supernatural ministry.

The truth is, God still intervenes supernaturally today. Thankfully and mercifully, I can testify to the fact. Besides His presence entering my room when I was a young teenager to offer me His friendship, I have had a few more supernatural encounters with this awesome God and His angels.

One time in my life, I seriously considered suicide. I was nineteen years old and had just recently switched from studying B Med Sc. to theology at university. I was about six or seven months into my theology studies and life was hard. My parents were terribly disappointed by the switch, and they made their disapproval known at every opportunity. Today I realize they were just trying to be responsible parents. They were afraid for my future, as women were not allowed on the pulpit of the Dutch Reformed Church at the time. They were concerned about how I was going to pay student loans and live if I couldn't get work once I completed my studies. Every phone call and every visit turned into either an argument or a flat out fight, with my dad exploding just about every time. They also withdrew their support to a great degree, forcing me to work full-time as a teller in a bank while attending classes at night. To be fair, though, they really couldn't afford to carry me and my studies and I gave them very little incentive to even try. My mom, who made a career out of banking, tried to persuade me at every opportunity to make banking my career and leave the "nonsense" of theology alone. She was the reason I was working in the bank to begin with.

My parents' friends got on the bandwagon too. I started receiving phone calls from some of them to chastise me for causing such grief to my parents. After all, me, a woman, wanting to be a pastor in the Dutch Reformed Church, was utter nonsense! They saw it as their duty to try to bully some sense into me for my parents' sake.

Working at the bank wasn't fun either. My mom had connections through the bank, and she let the administrative manager and the head bank manager know how deeply concerned she and my dad were about my ridiculous choice to study theology. She requested that they talk some sense into me, which they tried to do. I had to sit through numerous "fatherly" lectures in the bank manager's office about the fact that I should start acting responsibly and making better choices.

University itself was a cold, unfriendly place too. I found it hard to fit in anywhere. Before I switched directions, God's calling was weighing very heavily on me, threatening to strangle the life out of me. Failing grades didn't help any either. After I switched directions, almost everywhere I went, when students found out what I was studying, they frowned upon me. I was swimming upstream against a strong current of condemnation and disapproval. Much later, God showed me that He called it pioneering; almost everybody else called it stupidity!

In order to avoid the pain of rejection, I withdrew more and more. I became the ultimate loner, allowing only a handful of people close to my heart. Loneliness and rejection became painful, constant companions until finally, on one particular day, they almost destroyed me.

I sat on my bed, distraught. The isolation, loneliness and rejection were crushing me. Of course today I know and understand that this was the enemy's ploy. In my handbag I had a licensed .32 short-nosed Llama revolver, which I carried for self-protection. I took it out of my handbag and put it on the bed next to me. I was literally intoxicated—but not with drugs or alcohol. I didn't take drugs, and I didn't drink. I was totally sober, and yet intoxicated . . . with grief. Some would call it depression. Years later, I found out it was really demonic oppression. Life had taken its toll, and loneliness and rejection had broken my spirit and robbed me of all hope and joy as well as the will to live. Really, a spirit of intimidation was on assignment to oppress and persecute me, and I was caving in.

I had lain down beside that revolver in a fetal position, contemplating using it on myself, when I fell into a deep trance; it was almost like I had become unconscious or blacked out. Today I have quite a vivid memory of looking down at myself and the revolver on the bed. Did I actually leave my body during that blackout, or do I just have a vivid imagination? I wish I could explain it. All I know is, I desired with all my heart to die.

Suddenly, in that unconscious state, a loud, crisp, sharp, female voice shouted my name. I was jolted completely awake by the voice and an alarming realization of what I was contemplating. My whole body was trembling from the shock of it all, and I knew beyond a shadow of a doubt that an angel of the Lord had just saved my life. I shudder to think of the consequences had I remained in that trance-like state. Shaken and sober, with the aftermath of the angel's voice still ringing in my ears, I put the revolver back in my handbag. Never again did I contemplate suicide. Like I said, God does still intervene supernaturally.

God also intervenes through people.

"But he said, 'Please, Lord, now send the message by whomever You will.' Then the anger of the LORD burned against Moses, and He said, 'Is there not your brother Aaron the Levite? I know that he speaks fluently. And moreover, behold, he is coming out to meet you; when he sees you, he will be glad in his heart. You are to speak to him and put the words in his mouth; and I, even I, will be with your mouth and his mouth, and I will teach you what you are to do. Moreover, he shall speak for you to the people; and he will be as a mouth for you and you will be as God to him.'" – Exodus 4:13-16

When God drafts a person, there is no saying no. As I've already written elsewhere, most people get free will, except those who get drafted. Saul can tell you all about being drafted in Acts 9:6 where he finds himself confronted and blinded by Jesus and is told to *"get up and enter the city, and it will be told you what you must do."*

After spending the past forty years sojourning, not hearing from God, and sort of establishing himself in Midian, Moses tried every excuse in the book to get out of this assignment; but all he received in return was God's anger. However, God did have mercy on Moses. Since the assignment seemed too hard for Moses, God relented and said that he would assign Moses' brother as his mouthpiece. Aaron would become his right-hand man and help him to accomplish the assignment. All of a sudden, Aaron was drafted too. As a matter of fact, Aaron was already on his way and Israel's day of salvation was on their way. Hmm . . . is Isaiah 49:8 true or what? God's got you covered. No more excuses!

So, God put some people in my life . . .

God gives me a mentor called Ann.

I guess my very serious contemplation of suicide was my way of trying to say no because I felt the assignment was too hard. God knew it, and He already had a person in place to come alongside me to help me accomplish my assignment, just like Aaron coming alongside Moses. Her name was Ann, and she was the City Physician, a mother of four teenage boys and wife to a specialist physician and professor on the medical faculty of the university. She was driven, intelligent, organized, successful and influential, immaculately dressed, a modern career woman, but also a devoted mother and wife with a pastor's heart. I met Ann through my parents who knew her parents. Both our parents lived in the town where I grew up, and because I was initially aspiring to become a doctor, my parents suggested I meet Ann and her husband. They were both doctors and lived in the city where I was going to attend med school.

I'm not quite sure how our friendship developed, though, except that it was a "God thing." I never did tell her or anybody else about the suicide incident. I was a teenager just barely holding it together, and she was an accomplished professional woman. What could she possibly see in me? Like I said, it was a "God thing." God assigned her to be a strong, motherly mentor to me, and somehow she accepted, although I know that at times she would rather not have. The fact that she already had four teenagers to deal with didn't make it easy to kind of "adopt" another one. Her family didn't always appreciate my presence either. I wasn't exactly lovable, and with everybody's busy schedules, it was already hard for them to have private family time. My presence often encroached on their privacy.

I marvel at the fact that she stuck with me all the way through my nine years at university, and I marvel even more that we are still friends today. Today she is retired and an accomplished author on top of all her other accomplishments; in fact, she edited the first draft of this book as I wrote it. I don't think she had any idea what a lifeline she was to this lonely teenager. When I was close to her, I felt secure and safe; and when I threatened to unravel, she sternly and lovingly kept me on task. If I tried to take shortcuts, she would make it very clear that "anything worth doing is worth doing well." She also made it clear that she didn't back losing horses, so I was therefore expected to accomplish my goals at university. She was a tough lady with a pastor's heart.

I think it's also important to mention that Ann's presence in my life did not negate my parents, although I think they sometimes felt she did. Looking back, I realize that I simply needed a mentor in my life who understood some of the path I had to walk. My parents neither finished high school nor went to university, though they still excelled in their work because they are intelligent people. My dad ended his career in mining by completing a project that was pure engineering, and my mom completed her career in the bank as the administrative manager's assistant. They accomplished great things but, the fact was, they couldn't advise me on aspects of navigating university life and being a woman in a stereotypical man's world. Ann could. Both theology and medicine were stereotypically male oriented.

When Ann had studied to become a doctor, women doctors were not that respected. She understood some of the persecution that came with a profession that didn't appreciate women. In spite of her being a woman, though, she eventually became the City Physician in the capital city of our province, a position with political and community influence. This was no small feat. God knew what He was doing when He picked her as my mentor.

Several people blessed me in various ways, and I'm very thankful for their love and devotion; even my parents tried their best, albeit through a lot of conflict. Besides my parents and Ann, two more people, two more "Aarons," Sheila and Anthony, played pivotal roles in God's grace to get me through university.

Sheila

I was twenty years old and had just moved to a small farm on the outskirts of the city, yet another cause of concern for my parents. By this time, they were pulling their hair out in utter frustration over my irresponsible decisions. They felt that I was unnecessarily exposing myself to danger by living on a small farm. From my perspective, it came down to budget restrictions. It was cheaper to live there, and I had to make every penny count.

I had been there about a month when I heard a knock at the door one Saturday morning. I opened it, and in front of me stood a black Sotho tribal lady. I estimated her to be somewhere in her late fifties or early sixties. Despite the fact that seSotho was her mother language, she declared confidently in perfect Afrikaans that the Lord had sent her to be my maid and take care of me.

I was speechless for a moment, but gathered myself together and explained to her that there was no way I could afford a maid as I was just barely making ends meet. Having a maid wasn't anywhere on my radar. Sheila was undeterred. She said she had a calling from the Lord, and He would provide. There was no arguing with this lady, and Sheila moved into the maid's quarters, which was a separate building outside, that very day.

At first I was concerned that she and her family were destitute and that she was using a so-called "calling" as a way to get a roof over their heads; but as time progressed, she proved herself to be the real deal. Maybe she was destitute, but she meant it when she said that she had a calling from

God to take care of me, and she was right about God providing. Somehow I managed to pay her something every month.

Sheila gave me breakfast in bed every morning, my clothes were washed and ironed, my shoes shone like mirrors, the house was a dream of organization and cleanliness, and I got the tastiest hot meals every night when I arrived home. If I came home after working a full day at the bank and even suggested that I was going to skip class that night because I was too tired, Sheila would have a fit. She would literally push me out the door; and if that didn't work, she would walk down to the end of the driveway, open the gates and just stand there waiting for me to get my act together. Occasionally there were times when we ran out of groceries, but still somehow Sheila managed to put something on the dinner table. Ann also made sure that I got fed whenever I went to her house. Can angels come in human form?

I was on a lonely, hard pilgrimage, and God sent this unlikely servant-companion-parent figure into my life who kept me encouraged and on task. It reminded me of Elijah and the widow. Of all the people God could have sent, he sent a destitute Black widowed maid to take care of me. And did she ever take care of me . . . often better than she did her own family. Sheila also acted as my translator when I preached to Black tribal people. And the reason I was safe on that farm was because of her presence—she was a type of tribal matriarch. The Black tribal people respected and feared her. This Black tribal matriarch listened to the still small voice of the Lord to take care of a young White woman in the midst of hate and murder that was perpetuated by segregation and racism. She's one of the most amazing people I ever met.

Anthony

Six long years had passed since I started my studies. I was twenty-three years old and completing the last year of my first degree, which I had done by taking classes part-time while working. However, the Dutch Reformed

Church required two degrees in theology before you could be ordained, the second degree being part of Seminary. The Church's seminary was an actual theology faculty at the university, and the church took great pride in the fact that all its pastors were highly educated and that theologians from all across the world, even America, came there to either lecture or study. We were constantly reminded that we had the same quality training that a doctor would have. The only problem was that, when doctors went into practice, they generated three or four times the income a pastor did, but pastors left university with the same amount of student debt that a doctor did. It took some pastors fifteen to twenty years to pay off their student loans.

I was wrapping up my first degree with the realization that I had a problem. I couldn't attend seminary on a part-time basis. It was a three-year full-time degree consisting of classes in the mornings with mountains of homework for the afternoons and evenings, and we also had to do active voluntary ministry work in our local churches. During the last two years of seminary, we were also expected to relieve pastors during vacation times in their respective congregations, so that we could get firsthand experience at pastoring a congregation. This meant that I couldn't work in the bank. How was I going to support myself? I had a grant from the church synod and a student loan at the bank, but that only covered my studies. What about normal everyday living costs like rent, utilities, food, clothes, etc.?

As I approached the end of the last year of my first degree, I resigned myself to the fact that I had come to the end of the line. Everybody who had frowned on me had been right. I had wasted my time. So, I accepted a higher paying position as a teller in a different bank, and I cancelled my church grant at the synod for the following year. Needless to say, my mom and dad were elated because finally my mom could get me to make banking a career. She was already dreaming of me writing bank exams and climbing the corporate ladder. I, on the other hand, felt deflated and totally unexcited about the future . . . but I was resigned. I still had one subject left before attaining my first degree, and so my plan was to finish it and be satisfied with the one degree. In spite of this one subject hanging in the balance, I had enough credits to allow me to start seminary when the new school year began in January. In South Africa, the school year was roughly from middle January to the end of November with three short breaks in between.

There I was, sitting in my rental home trying to get seminary out of my mind and accept the fact that I wouldn't be a pastor after all. The Dutch Reformed Church still didn't allow women in the ministry, so what was I thinking in any case? I was obviously mistaken about my calling.

God apparently didn't agree. The phone rang, and when I answered, a man on the other side said, "You don't know me, but I have a question for you. What is your greatest desire in life?" My first inclination was to put the phone down, but before I could help myself, I just blurted out, "To go to seminary and become a pastor." The voice on the other side replied, "You have answered well. My name is Anthony, and I have heard about your calling through my aunt. I am prepared to carry you financially while you attend seminary."

Anthony's aunt was a dear friend of mine and, unbeknownst to me, she was very burdened by the fact that I was not going to seminary. She was praying earnestly about it when the Lord laid it on her heart to approach Anthony to help me. Anthony was an optometrist with his own practice in Namibia, a country just northwest of South Africa. He told me that at first her request did not resonate with him at all, but he just couldn't get it out of his mind.

To make a long story short, Anthony paid all my personal expenses for three years while I went to seminary. The church synod had somehow never cancelled my grant, so it was still in my name and available, and the bank was happy to extend my student loan. I had to apologize deeply to the Lord for my lack of faith. I had allowed the slavery and pharaoh mindsets around me and in me to persuade me to give up on my dream . . . or was it His dream. Did I mention I was drafted? Mercifully, by the grace of God, in spite of my unbelief, God still made it happen. He does still intervene!

In spite of Moses throwing every excuse he could think of at God, through a burning bush and through Aaron, God supernaturally made it happen. Moses' calling was reinstated. In spite of my unbelief, through a grant that had somehow never been cancelled and through Anthony and his aunt's persistence, God supernaturally reinstated my calling.

Take time right now to ask Holy Spirit to teach you what it means for you specifically to "abide in Christ" and to have "His Word abide in you." Write down whatever comes to mind after you pray that prayer. How can you change and improve your circumstances with this newfound knowledge? Do you really believe that He will intervene, or do you believe that He's somewhere up there and you're somewhere down here trying to make it on your own?

"Now the LORD said to Abram, 'Go forth from your country, And from your relatives And from your father's house, To the land which I will show you; And I will make you a great nation, And I will bless you, And make your name great; And so you shall be a blessing; And I will bless those who bless you, And the one who curses you I will curse. And in you all the families of the earth will be blessed.'" – Genesis 12:1-3

"And God remembered his covenant with Abraham, Isaac and Jacob." – Exodus 2:24

God really is a covenant God and His ways are not our ways!

CHAPTER 6

"I Am Who I Am—The Lord"

"Then Moses said to God, 'Behold, I am going to the sons of Israel, and I will say to them, "The God of your fathers has sent me to you." Now they may say to me, "What is His name?" What shall I say to them?' God said to Moses, 'I AM WHO I AM'; and He said, 'Thus you shall say to the sons of Israel, "I AM has sent me to you."' God, furthermore, said to Moses, 'Thus you shall say to the sons of Israel, "The LORD, the God of your fathers, the God of Abraham, the God of Isaac, and the God of Jacob, has sent me to you." This is My name forever, and this is My memorial-name to all generations.'" – Exodus 3:13-15

Just before the above conversation took place, Moses was lured to a burning bush that just kept on burning (Exodus 3:2). Moses would have been used to seeing burning bushes in the desert, but they would have been quickly consumed. This one just kept on burning strongly. It was so strange and obviously burning for such an abnormal length of time, that Moses left his flock for a moment to investigate. I can just imagine him cautiously approaching the burning bush with all his senses zoomed in on it, trying to figure out why it wasn't being consumed by the fire when, out of the bush, a voice calls his name not once, but twice. "Moses, Moses" (Exodus 3:4). Boy! Spooky! I'm not sure whether I would have fainted or run at that moment. I might have just dropped dead from fright. Just ask Daniel; he knows what I'm talking about (Daniel 10:7-9).

God gets Moses' attention through an ordinary event turned extraordinary! It was ordinary because a burning bush was a familiar sight in the desert. It was extraordinary because the bush didn't burn up. Moses' ordinary life was about to make an abrupt, extraordinary change of course. That which started out as an ordinary day turned into a miraculous, extraordinary visitation. On an ordinary day, God leads him through ordinary circumstances to a very special place, God's mountain, to an extraordinary event that sets a scenario in motion that would change his life, his family's life and the course of history forever.

Maybe ordinary isn't as boring and bad as some people might want us to believe. Ordinary circumstances can lead to extraordinary revelation. So, my friend, don't despise the "ordinary" in your life. Maybe it's a good idea to embrace it and run with it and expect God to do extraordinary things through it.

After all, it is God who orchestrates the extraordinary, not you or me. God orchestrated an encounter with Moses when Moses least expected it or most probably didn't have such an expectation at all. Suddenly he was confronted with the ultimate surprise—I AM WHO I AM! Kind of reminds me of what Jesus said about the end times in Matthew 24:36-51. Let me highlight verse 44 here: *"For the Son of Man is coming at an hour when you do not think He will."* Are you ready to meet Him, my friend? He has an appointment with you whether you're expecting it or not, whether you believe or not.

This was no accidental meeting between God and Moses. God purposely looked up Moses, just as I believe Jesus purposely looked me up in my bedroom when I was a teenager. It's also important to note that God knew Moses by name. He called Moses twice by his name so that there could be no misunderstanding as to whom God was speaking. Jesus extrapolates on this personal side of God in John 10:27 when He states that He, Jesus, God Himself, has the same personal relationship with us: *"My sheep hear My voice, and I know them and they follow Me."*

The one and only great "I AM" is a personal God who doesn't mind getting involved in our ordinary daily lives, who actually doesn't mind getting right up into our faces at times. He is a relational God who tangibly meets Moses in real time. This was a real experience for Moses. It was not a dream. It was not an act of his imagination. It was tangibly real.

It's interesting to note that throughout the Bible and throughout the history of mankind right up to this modern day, whenever this Covenant God sent somebody on a specific mission from Him, He first orchestrated some kind of supernatural meeting with that person. All of these individuals have a testimony of God's supernatural world colliding with their ordinary natural world and changing their lives and the lives around them forever. Just a few examples to get you thinking are Biblical figures like Adam, Abraham, Gideon, David, Solomon, Ezekiel, Elijah, Moses, Daniel and the disciples in the New Testament; we also see this in modern-day figures like William Branham, Smith Wigglesworth, Maria Woodworth-Etter, Kathrine Kuhlman, Wesley, and so many more.

Each encounter with each of these individuals was different. For Moses, it resulted in an extraordinary ongoing relationship with God. From this supernatural point of contact forward, there was never anything vague between God and Moses again. God spoke plainly to him in a straightforward fashion (Exodus 33:11, Numbers 12:7-8). From this point onwards, Moses always knew exactly what God wanted, and if he didn't understand something altogether, all he had to do was ask and God readily explained it. What an awesome privilege to know the great "I AM," the

"Ancient of Days," on such a personal level. John tells us in John 15:7 that we too can have such a relationship with Him: *"If you abide in Me, and My words abide in you, ask whatever you wish, and it will be done for you."*

Have you started meditating on what Jesus actually means when He says to *"abide in Me and My words abide in you"*? What exactly does such a relationship between you and Jesus look like on a day-to-day basis? Please, stop and think about it . . . often. Start asking and continue asking the Holy Spirit to show you how to persistently and consistently enter into the truth of John 15:7. God gives salvation to us on a platter, but becoming one with the heart of the living God of the Covenant is a costly and rewarding journey.

It is time the church, God's children, you and I, pursued a relationship with Christ as described in John 15. Moses and John and many others are living testimonies that such relationship is attainable, and it is our heritage in Christ. We owe it to Christ to be a Moses and a John and a Jesus and a Solomon and a William Branham and a Smith Wigglesworth, and a . . . (fill your name in) . . . to the nations of this world, to our own environment, and to be faithful right to the very end, unlike Solomon who fell into sin towards the end of his life.

We owe it to Christ to represent His kingdom and His righteousness (Matthew 6:33) on this earth until we breathe our last breath. *"All authority has been given to Me [Christ] in heaven and on earth. Go, therefore, and make disciples of all the nations, baptizing them in the name of the Father and the Son and the Holy Spirit, teaching them to observe all that I commanded you, and lo, I am with you always, even to the end of the age"* (Matthew 28:18-20). *"And as you go, preach, saying, 'The kingdom of heaven is at hand.' Heal the sick, raise the dead, cleanse the lepers, cast out demons. Freely you received, freely give"* (Matthew 10:7-8). *"Therefore, if you have been raised up with Christ, keep seeking the things above, where Christ is, seated on the right hand of God. Set your mind on the things above, not on the things that are on earth"* (Colossians 3:1-2).

Verses like Colossians 3:1 and 2 should become a lifestyle, which should catapult us into the reality of verses like John 15:7. Jesus was so heavenly minded that He transformed earth to look like heaven. He prayed and believed and demonstrated *"Your kingdom come, your will be done. On earth as it is in heaven"* (Matthew 6:10). And then He promised, *"Truly, truly, I say to you, he who believes in Me, the works that I do, he will do also; and greater works than these he will do; because I go to the Father. Whatever you ask in My name, that will I do"* (John 14:12-13).

Sid Roth likes to start his television program with the following greeting, "Welcome to my world where it is naturally supernatural." Randy Clark also likes to teach about being naturally supernatural. I want to give it a twist and state that natural is being supernatural, because supernatural is God's natural; and if we are in Christ and Christ in us then . . . hopefully you get the picture. Moses cringed at the idea (Exodus 3:11). It seems as though the church is still cringing at the idea today. It is time, church! It is time to know who we are in Christ.

Who am I?

"But Moses said to God, 'Who am I, that I should go to Pharaoh, and that I should bring the sons of Israel out of Egypt?'" – Exodus 3:11

This is a very different Moses compared to the Moses that intervened on behalf of the slave and ended up killing an Egyptian soldier in the process. The Moses that killed the Egyptian soldier was a well-educated, eloquent and powerful Egyptian prince. The writer of Acts 7:20 wrote that, *"Moses [the Egyptian prince] was educated in all the learning of the Egyptians, and he was a man of power in words and deeds."*

The Moses at the burning bush seems to be a totally different Moses. He says to God in Exodus 4:10, "Please, Lord, I have never been eloquent, neither recently nor in time past, nor since You have spoken to Your servant; for I am slow of speech and slow of tongue."

Whatever happened to the Egyptian prince? Based on my own experience, I want to say, "Life happened." I have found out that life sometimes has a way of humbling some people to a point where they actually undergo such a metamorphosis that they can't even remember the person they used to be. Trauma can very easily obliterate memories and abilities and reduce people to mere ashes of their previous self, yours truly included. The question is, are those ashes always a reduction or can they actually be a promotion? Had the Egyptian prince been reduced, or was he actually promoted to a humble sojourner? The writer of Numbers 12:3 described Moses the sojourner as *"very humble, more than any man who was on the face of the earth."* The powerful, eloquent prince had been reduced to ashes, but the man, Moses, had been promoted to the greatest form of humbleness on the face of the earth. Could it be this quality that set Moses apart and put him in an intimate friendship with God, making him the most powerful man in the world of his time?

Moses saw himself as somebody reduced to ashes. "Who am I?" God saw him as somebody humbled and worthy to change the world. Saul underwent this same metamorphosis as he morphed into Paul the Apostle, and he had this to say about the process of reduction in Philippians 3:7, *"But whatever things were gain for me, those things I have counted as loss for the sake of Christ . . . for whom I have suffered the loss of all things, and count them but rubbish so that I may gain Christ, and may be found in Him, not having a righteousness of my own . . . but . . . the righteousness that comes from God on the basis of faith."*

"Who am I?" This question haunts every Christian going through hardships and so many fail to come up with the right answer. So many choose to be horrified by the ashes around them and in them instead of being impressed by the Sovereign God they serve in the midst of whatever they are going through. So many allow themselves to be reduced to the facts of the stormy moment in which they find themselves, instead of mentally and spiritually staying the course in Christ and in the truth of His Word in the midst of that stormy moment. *"If you abide in Me, and My words abide in you, ask whatever you wish, and it will be done for you."*

Instead of abiding in Christ and His Promises, so many choose to abide in the facts of the challenges that life throws at them. Instead of professing the truths of the Bible and the faithfulness of God during hardships, so many choose to profess the hopelessness of their difficult situations . . . "Who am I?"

Am I a victim of circumstances reduced to ashes, just surviving and of no use to anybody because I'm just barely holding on? I've been there and thought that. How about you? Am I a positive thinker, who, by mere positive thoughts, has some success in overcoming, but never really totally overcomes, because one day I can actually be positive and overcome and another I fall apart because I just can't get myself to be positive that day? Positive thinking is good; it's at least a step up from the victim mentality, but it does not have longevity.

However, there is another answer to the question, "Who am I?" I am the product of a life in Christ, and I can change the world in and through Him in spite of difficulties. By consistently abiding in Him and His Word in me, even through the dark and difficult times, I can eventually be promoted to that place in Christ where the ceiling is lifted to my possibilities in Christ on this earth, where I can live from the heart and authority of Christ to change my environment and bring it into alignment with the kingdom of Christ, where the Joseph mindset gets promoted to a life immersed in Christ in partnership with Holy Spirit.

The church has yet to embrace her full identity in Christ.

"And I, brethren, could not speak to you as to spiritual men, but as to men of flesh, as to infants in Christ. I gave you milk to drink, not solid food; for you were not yet able to receive it. Indeed, even at the present you are not yet able, for you are still fleshly. For since there is jealousy and strife among you, are you not walking like mere men?" – 1 Corinthians 3:1-3

Except for two people, Joshua and Caleb, an entire generation died in the wilderness after leaving Egypt, because they just couldn't let go of their slavery and pharaoh mindsets which were rooted in Egypt; and they could not, would not, embrace a new identity in the God of the Covenant. Even Moses eventually succumbed to their rebelliousness and disobeyed God in a fit of rage, disqualifying himself from entering the Promised Land.

In this context, it is important to note that the Promised Land does not refer to heaven, as so many Christians like to understand it. Moses died in that wilderness and went to heaven, but he never got to enter the Promised Land that was available to him on this earth. In a New Testament context, the Promised Land refers to that place in Christ that John talks about. It is the place where individuals abide in Christ and His Word in them, and they literally become united partners with Holy Spirit, establishing the kingdom of God and His righteousness on this earth as it is in heaven in the name of Jesus.

The Promised Land, in our context today, refers to the Joseph mindsets of Joshua and Caleb crossing the Jordan of persistent abiding in Christ and His Word in them, to eventually be transformed into the likeness of Christ where the sick are healed, the dead are raised, the demons are cast out, the lepers are cleansed and greater things are done than Jesus did. It is the place where Caleb gets his mountain and Joshua gets to lead an entire new generation into a victorious partnership with the living "I AM," and it all happens in the land of milk and honey, which is the kingdom of God tangibly demonstrated *"on earth as it is in heaven"* (Matthew 6:10).

Jesus preached according to Matthew 4:17, *"Repent for the kingdom of heaven is at hand."* I listened to Bill Johnson explain in a sermon that "repent" means to change your thinking. Let go of the old and embrace the new in Christ. Joyce Meyers likes to say that we need to get rid of our "stinking thinking" and replace it with heavenly thinking. Jesus said, "repent." Why? The answer is simple and profound, *"The kingdom of heaven is at hand."* The kingdom mindset is where Christ is, but where is the church? Is she still stuck in 1 Corinthians 3:1-3? *"And I, brethren, could not speak to you as to spiritual men, but as to men of flesh, as to infants in Christ. I gave you milk to drink, not solid food; for you were not yet able to receive it. Indeed, even now you are not yet able, for you are still fleshly. For since there is jealousy and strife among you, are you not fleshly, and are you not walking like mere men?"*

The church as a corporate entity has to change her thinking, change her behavior, let go of old mindsets. It is time for the church to graduate into that place in Christ where she can become a people with a kingdom mindset. I applaud the current day Calebs and Joshuas who are faithfully pursuing the kingdom mindset, but it seems to me that the corporate body called the church is lagging behind, dying in the wilderness of her fleshliness. Just like Moses at the burning bush, she's vehemently trying to avoid doing the things Jesus did and greater things by offering every theological excuse she can find and majoring in her carnality (fleshliness) instead of her spirituality. "Who are you, church?" "Who am I?" Is your identity wrapped up in your flesh, or is it wrapped up in Christ? One leads to death. The other leads to abundant, victorious, supernatural, life-giving vitality.

Christ is greater than . . .

"All authority has been given to Me [Christ] in heaven and on earth." – Matthew 28:18

What part of "all authority" do we not understand? Why is it that when a proverbial Delilah, some form of crisis, enters our lives, we end up under the juniper tree like Elijah, wishing we were dead? Since when does the proverbial Delilah, our crisis, have more authority than Jesus? Luke couldn't have stated it any clearer than he did in Luke 1:37 when he said, "For with God **nothing** shall be impossible."

Nothing or nobody can override the authority of Christ in our lives—not terminal illness, not financial turmoil, not natural disasters, not social injustices, not anything. The Lord, the great I AM, Jesus Christ Himself, is a wall of fire around us and the glory in our midst (Zechariah 2:5). Isaiah 54:17 tells us, *"No weapon that is formed against you will prosper."* I want to lovingly submit that we perish because we either don't understand this or we don't really believe it or we're too timid to embrace it. Who are you, church? Who am I? *"Truly, truly, I say to you, he who believes in Me, the works that I do, he will do also; and greater works than these he will do; because I go to the Father. Whatever you ask in My name, that will I do"* (John 14:12-13).

Let me revisit Hosea 4:6, which states that we perish for a lack of knowledge. That word *knowledge* is not referring to academic knowledge; it is referring to Holy Spirit revelation. It is referring to the process that occurs when information travels from your mind to your heart and Holy Spirit transforms your way of doing and thinking. You can't just read and study Scriptures like John 14 and 15 and think you've done your duty. You have to assimilate it, become it!

Holy Spirit dishes it up, but you have to eat it, digest it, absorb it into every fiber of your being. Then, through a lively, real relationship with Holy Spirit, you have to live it, courageously, without doubt; you must keep eating it and keep digesting it and keep absorbing it and keep living it, courageously, until it happens, refusing to accept anything less. This process of assimilation requires steadfast resolve: *"For that man [the one who doubts] ought not to expect that he will receive anything from the Lord"* (James 1:7). It requires determination and courage: *"Be strong and coura- geous!"* (Joshua 1:5-9). It requires an absolute, undeterred focus on Jesus Christ: *"fixing our eyes on Jesus . . ."* (Hebrews 12:1-2). This is all rooted in trust. If you can't trust Jesus and His promises in the Bible even when your situation seems hopeless, then you will not be able to live this way.

Lastly, it often requires seasoning, a process of maturing in Christ, which takes time—this kind of faith does not happen overnight. Moses was eighty years old at the burning bush event, and Joshua and Caleb were each eighty years old when they finally crossed the Jordan into the Promised Land. The seasoning process is different for each individual; however, there does come a time when you either cross the Jordan or you perish.

Church, it is time to cross over! Are you going to be a Joshua and a Caleb, or are you going to perish in your wilderness of fleshliness and miss out on

God's highest for you and through you? Just know this: the Joshuas and the Calebs will go forth with or without you. I believe a new corporate generation of church is rising up out of the Joseph mindset, seasoned by the challenges of the wilderness, totally seated in Christ, ready to bring heaven to earth, ready to do the things Jesus did and greater things on a scale that will literally transform nations into the likeness of Jesus Christ. The John 15 generation of church, the Joshua and the Caleb, is approaching her Jordan. By God's grace, may you and I be part of that generation. Are you coming, church?

Pray and decree and live truth until it happens.

"Let us not lose heart in doing good, for in due time we will reap if we do not grow weary." – Galatians 6:9

I am often asked, "How long must I pray for *xyz*? I've been praying for years with no results. How much longer?" Even strong Biblical figures of faith like David asked this question. Read Psalm 13. The answer is simple. You pray and believe and don't doubt and do whatever the Lord leads you to do until it happens or until He says no or until you go to be with the Lord in heaven. You either trust God and His Word or you don't.

To illustrate, let's look at Psalm 41:3 which states, *"The Lord will sustain him upon his sickbed. In his illness, You restore him to health."* Let's say you're deathly ill while reading this verse. You now have a choice. You can assimilate and believe the diagnosis and prognosis of your illness, or you can assimilate and believe Psalm 41:3. You can spend all day rehearsing the facts that the doctors have told you about your illness, or you can use every symptom as a reason to profess Psalm 41:3 and other verses of healing.

You can believe and live and rehearse the facts, or you can believe and rehearse the Truth until you are healed, until your body and your life lines up with the Truth and you start living the Truth again. And even if healing doesn't come, you keep professing just like Habakkuk, *"Though the fig tree should not blossom and there be no fruit on the vines, though the yield of the olive should fail and the fields produce no food, though the flock should be cut off from the fold and there be no cattle in the stalls, Yet I will exult in the Lord, I will rejoice in the God of my salvation. The Lord is my strength"* (Habakkuk 3:17-19). As I've mentioned before, this is not for the fainthearted. It requires courage and resolve and a single-minded focus on Jesus Christ: *"If you abide in Me, and My words abide in you, ask whatever you wish, and it will be done for you"* (John 15:7). It requires the conviction of Holy Spirit.

While I was writing chapter four of this book, just before our Thanksgiving holiday in the USA, I had an acute attack of diverticulitis. I knew it was diverticulitis because I have had a few similar attacks in years gone by. Interestingly, I was writing about circumstances in my life that used to bring these attacks to the forefront, and while writing and thinking about them, a major attack occurred. I had the whole nine yards of excruciating pain, fatigue that was so bad I could hardly put one foot in front of the other, and some things I'd rather not mention, but you get the picture. The acute part of the attack lasted for ten days, and the fatigue clung for three more months. It was probably one of the worst attacks I've had so far. In the past, I would go straight to the doctor, and I remember one particular incident when I was in tenth grade when I actually ended up in hospital for three days with such an attack. Had I gone to the doctor this time, I'm almost positive that he or she would have admitted me to the hospital.

However, this time I did not have the luxury of going to the doctor because I did not have insurance. As I prayed, though, the Lord gave me a revelation that this was a demonic attack. I received a very clear knowledge from Him that this was a test. The forces of darkness wanted to see if I really believed what I was writing. Instead of going to the doctor, the direction from the Lord was clear. I needed to do spiritual warfare. It was time to pull out my verses on healing and decree them over myself and exercise my faith in the Word. Romans 10:17 tells us, *"Faith comes by hearing and hearing by the word of Christ."*

When you are so tired that you actually want to throw up from being tired, and the pain is close to a ten on a scale of one to ten, then decreeing Scripture while you're trying to go about your daily business as best you can is not easy. And when you eventually start fighting dizziness as well and some real nausea and bloody stools, you either get gripped by fear or you apply faith with great resolve. Abiding in Christ and His Word in us does not imply that we ignore the "messy" and "ugly" in our lives; it implies we confront and overcome it in Christ.

For example, when you're fighting cancer or kidney failure or some other dreadful disease and fluid is filling your body and congestive heart failure is kicking in and you're vomiting your guts out—which is what friends of mine were fighting—it becomes a real, ugly, death-defying fight. However, in Christ, you have weapons that go beyond the natural, beyond the doctors and medicine and hospitals. *"Set your mind on the things above, not on the things that are on earth"* (Colossians 3:2).

It's important to note that the reason I did not go to the doctor was because I received a word, a revelation from the Lord. The fact that I did not have insurance made me pause in prayer long enough to hear from Him. Had He told me to see the doctor, I would have had to trust Him to provide the funds for it. So, I am not dismissing doctors; there have been other times where God told me to go. Part of living a life in Christ is listening for His guidance through Holy Spirit. In the midst of your illness, on your sickbed, in the midst of doctors and nurses and therapies and medicines, you also have supernatural means seated in a supernatural God. Paul tells us in 2 Corinthians 10:3, *"For though we walk in the flesh, we do not war according to the flesh, for the weapons of our warfare are not of the flesh, but divinely powerful for the destruction of fortresses."*

Based on 2 Corinthians 10:3 and other verses just like it, I believe that we can actually reach a level of faith in Christ where we can stop cancer and heart failure and kidney failure and every other disease right at its inception, before we even get to the doctor and hospital phase. I believe there is an entire generation of church arising that will live and demonstrate this truth. For now, I also believe it is available to any individual who is willing to go through God's pruning process of becoming one with Him and like Him in order to live a life that surrenders all of self for all of God.

"The Lord shall cause your enemies who rise up against you to be defeated before you. They will come out against you one way and will flee before you seven ways . . . So all the peoples of the earth will see that you are called by the name of the Lord and they will be afraid of you" (Deuteronomy 28:7, 10). *"Therefore I say to you, all things for which you pray and ask, believe that you have received them and they will be granted to you"* (Mark 11:24).

To get back to my story, seven months after that attack, I was healed! By God's grace, I abided in Christ and His Word in me, I decreed the Word every time I dealt with a symptom, which was practically all the time, and I resolved in my heart not to think about anything except victory in Jesus, *"for by His wounds you were healed"* (1 Peter 2:22). I am a walking testimony that I am healed by the wounds of Jesus Christ! Will I have to fight this fight again? Will the forces of darkness revisit this same scenario at another time? It's possible, but the Truth is, I've won! I believe that, sooner or later, diverticulitis and a spastic colon will no longer plague me because eventually the forces of darkness will get the message and quit. *"Submit therefore to God. Resist the devil and he will flee from you"* (James 4:7).

This victory is one more step towards my Jordan. I *will* do the things that Jesus did and greater things. I *will* heal the sick in Jesus' name. I'm not there yet, but I sure am not where I used to be either. *I'm on my way,* as Joyce Meyers likes to say!

Who are you, church? Who am I? You and I are children of the living God, redeemed by Jesus Christ, filled and empowered by His Holy Spirit, called to represent His kingdom and His righteousness on this earth.

We are a friend and representative of the great "I AM" in Christ Jesus.
"God said to Moses, 'I AM WHO I AM ' . . . Thus you shall say to the sons of Israel, 'I AM has sent me to you.'" – Exodus 3:14

We are friends with and represent the great "I AM" who has no beginning and no end, the God who cannot be fully defined by human words or terms. "I AM" is the one and only living God who, by the way, is the same yesterday, today and forever (Hebrews 13:8). He is the God of the Covenant, and the Covenant is just as relevant today as it was the moment of its inception with Abraham. The Covenant was born through Abraham and finally culminated and brought to full power and full meaning in and through Jesus Christ (Matthew 5:17). The great "I AM" is a personal God who created life, redeemed life and is still involved in life as we know it. He is faithful, consistent and stable. He does not compromise, and He cannot be manipulated by evil. He is "I AM WHO I AM."

He is "the Lord"!

"Thus you shall say to the sons of Israel, 'The Lord, the God of your fathers, the God of Abraham, the God of Isaac, and the God of Jacob, has sent me to you.' This is My name forever, and this is My memorial-name to all generations.'" – Exodus 3:15

"The Lord" is His *"memorial-name to all generations,"* to all colors and creeds, to all nations and languages, to all ages. The name "The Lord" implies that He is the Creator; He has full authority in heaven and on earth, He is almighty, all powerful, omniscient, sovereign . . . He is above all things and all people and all leaders, a lesson Pharaoh was about to learn with grave consequences. He is the King of the universe, and He demands respect and obedience and worship and acknowledgement. He is a jealous God. *"You shall have no other gods before Me"* (Exodus 20:3). He is also thoroughly involved in your life and mine as a redeemer and provider (Exodus 3:9, Psalm 30:2, 2 Corinthians 9:10-11).

I can summarize the above with one admonition, "Don't mess with The Lord!" Many have learned this lesson the hard way, even died because of it. We're going to get to Pharaoh in a little bit, but other people like Moses and Paul and Herod can attest to this with great clarity.

Herod

"The people kept crying out, 'The voice of a god and not of a man!' And immediately an angel of the Lord struck him because he did not give God the glory, and he was eaten by worms and died." – Acts 12:22-23

Herod is an example of a political leader that God actually took out because he threatened the survival of the early church by persecuting and executing Christians; and when the crowds exalted him to the status of a god, he relished in their adoration and embraced the title of god, denying that there was only one God. Sounds a lot like Pharaoh, doesn't it? Playing god in peoples' lives might bring temporary fame and fortune, but it is a suicidal mission. Just ask satan himself.

Saul who became the apostle Paul

"Saul got up from the ground, and though his eyes were open, he could see nothing." – Acts 9:8

Saul was zealously defending Jewish traditions and the Jewish faith, and he saw the Christians as heretics. According to his thinking, they were blaspheming God and therefore needed to be put to death. In today's terms, Saul would be called an extreme activist for his beliefs. Some might even call him a terrorist. He wanted to destroy the Christian movement by annihilating every Christian he could find; and he had the law and the church of the day on his side. He was empowered to do this and, as a result, Saul posed a very real threat for the continuing existence of the emerging Christian church. She was still babyishly fragile and vulnerable. So God intervened on the road to Damascus.

He confronts this zealous Jewish Scribe with all His glory as the resurrected and ascended Christ, and the confrontation leaves Saul blind for three days. You reckon that got his attention? I wonder what would have happened if Saul had not been blinded for three days. Would he have shrugged off the event as imaginary and just continued with his tyranny? Saul was heavily handicapped for three days. He couldn't go where he wanted to go; he was forced to be totally dependent on others and to stop and think about this encounter. Saul, the powerful, bloodthirsty extremist, was supernaturally apprehended and put in a straightjacket of blindness by God himself. Herod was supernaturally killed, but Saul was supernaturally apprehended. I believe the difference between these two men was a heart issue. Herod exalted himself to the status of a god, while Saul sincerely thought he was serving the great "I AM" and therefore being obedient to His will. Herod was evil. Saul was misguided.

Saul had encountered the resurrected and ascended Christ and lived to tell the tale, but not without a price. Would he ever be able to see again? He already knew he couldn't go back to his old ways. No, no, no. All of a sudden, he had a new perspective on Christ and Christianity. After this supernatural encounter with Christ, he knew that Jesus was the Messiah and that his theology and belief system, his thinking, had to change. He had to repent!

I believe God kept him in that blind condition until he totally embraced the idea that Jesus was definitely the Messiah. This knowledge had to become revelation; it had to travel from the experience of the encounter to his heart, and he had to make massive paradigm shifts in his thinking. He had to become equally as zealous about following Christ as he was about persecuting and killing Christ and his followers.

Come to think of it, this just proves how powerful God is. It took Him only three days to transform this murderous man into a whole new humble individual complete with a new name, Paul. It took man a lifetime to develop and form Saul into one of the most sought after Pharisees and Synagogue leaders of his day. It took God only one encounter and three days to strip him of all of that and turn him into a humble piece of clay.

Moses

"Now it came about at the lodging place on the way that the Lord met him and sought to put him to death." – Exodus 4:24

After realizing that no excuse in the book was going to get him off the hook, Moses packed his goods and his family and took off to Egypt. On the way, though, God almost killed him. Being drafted to pioneer for God is serious business, and Moses needed some sobering up. He was going to represent the God of the Covenant, but his first born son and possibly Moses himself, failed to wear the sign of the Covenant. They weren't circumcised, and the story in Exodus 4:24-26 suggests that both he and his wife must have known that they had neglected this little detail, because when it came down to the wire, we read in Exodus 4:25 that his wife knew exactly what to do to save her husband from the wrath of God. She cut off her son's foreskin and threw it at Moses" feet. This word "feet" in the Hebrew language is often used as a euphemism for testicles. She threw it at Moses testicles.

Moses' wife was clearly shaken in the story, and I'm sure he was too. Being uncircumcised was just as bad as Pharaoh refusing to put blood on his doorposts the night his son died (Exodus 12:12-13, 29-30). Being uncircumcised left Moses and his family unprotected and outside of the Covenant. The message was clear. Moses was a pioneer drafted by God to navigate God's children through dangerous, treacherous territory on their way to the Promised Land. He had to learn very quickly that one wrong step or one act of disobedience from a pioneer could lead to death; something that became a sad reality when God denied him entrance into the Promised Land.

We see an incident in the New Testament where God kills two of his pioneers in Acts 5, because they didn't take God seriously. Their names were Ananias and Sapphira. They were part of the early church, pioneering the way of the kingdom of Christ. They were expected to set the bar high and maintain it there, but they thought a little white lie wouldn't hurt anybody. After all, who would know? Their deaths reverberated a clear message: Don't mess with "The Lord"!

The judge by the river

"Do not be dismayed before them, or I will dismay you before them." – Jeremiah 1:17

I, too, have had some very humbling and scary experiences with "The Lord." One particular season of my ministry in South Africa is etched deeply into my memory. I was in the midst of heavy conflict with several leaders in my congregation and community, as well as leaders of the Dutch Reformed Circuit that my congregation was part of, as well as groups of like-minded people inside and outside of the congregation, who insisted I only allow White Afrikaner people into our Sunday services as well as other church activities.

They wanted me to make an official announcement that all other races were not allowed in our church building for our worship services, Bible studies and other church activities. The fight for apartheid was lost on a political front, but they were bent on enforcing it on a religious front. The Dutch Reformed Church had led the case for apartheid right from its inception, and even though her leaders had backed down and announced that they were wrong about apartheid, this congregation and community was not going to submit without a fight.

Being a representative of Jesus Christ, I refused to enforce apartheid. With me, it had nothing to do with politics. Even if apartheid had continued to be "politically correct," I would still have refused, because I represented Jesus Christ and His Word. I did not represent a political ideology which had kidnapped Scripture to push its own agenda. This is when I found out firsthand just how evil mankind can be and just how much courage it took to be a pioneer for God and stay the course of obedience in the midst of danger and threats.

People threw bricks at my dog as they drove by the parsonage; others zoomed in on my grandmother who lived with me, an old woman in her eighties, doing great emotional damage and causing her to spiral into a terrible depression from which she never recovered. Others were a lot braver, attacking me directly with threatening phone calls and visits and confrontations. Others tried to get me fired by calling the seminary and accusing me of being a lesbian because I was single and ministering to some single women in the congregation. One group started a campaign against me by filing a formal complaint at the Circuit suggesting that I was unfit to lead that congregation. Suffice it to say, evil was having a heyday. It got to a point where I had no idea who was friend and who was foe. When I bemoaned these facts to the Lord during one quiet time, He gave me Jeremiah 1:17: *"Do not be dismayed before them, or I will dismay you before them."* That was it. End of discussion.

In the midst of this, I received a phone call from my parents. A judge, a representative of the law, had befriended them over time at different Saddlebred horse shows they attended, and he wanted to meet with me. He finally convinced them that he had my best interests at heart and wanted to help me. From the minute they told me who he was and where he wanted to meet me, I knew he represented trouble; but they just couldn't accept that a judge who represented the law could possibly be a bad person. Even they became threatening when at first I did not want to meet with him. I eventually conceded for their sake.

The judge wanted to meet me in my hometown where I grew up and where my parents still lived, and he wanted to meet me on the banks of the river where it would be private. Does this make your hairs raise? It did mine. My hometown had a pleasure resort on the banks of the river with a campsite, and he wanted to meet me at the campsite. When I got there, the campsite was deserted. It was just the two of us. Creepy!

What came out of his mouth was disgusting and shocking to say the least. Based on what he said, it was very clear to me that he represented an organization which consisted of a group of men who were the underground secret enforcers of apartheid during the apartheid era. I knew about this organization, but I had never come face to face with one of its representatives in such a revealing manner. The Dutch Reformed Church and the government had been in cahoots with each other since the inception of apartheid to convince the masses that apartheid was Biblical, and these men of this secret organization made sure that pastors preached apartheid from the pulpit or else.

I had heard in the corridors of seminary, while studying to be a minister, how these men persecuted and even physically hurt pastors and their families, and how they also got them fired or caused them to resign if they would not enforce apartheid in their congregations. Some pastors were even murdered, and others were driven to nervous breakdowns that institutionalized them if they refused to comply. Of course there's no proof of this because, just like the judge, these men made sure that their confrontations with these pastors and their families were private. These pastors are some of the unsung martyrs of the apartheid era.

After I resigned from the Dutch Reformed Church, some of these pastors actually reached out to me and shared their personal stories with me firsthand. I hadn't met these pastors and their families yet when I stood on the riverbank facing this judge, but I had heard stories; and now I was faced with the reality.

It became clear to me through him that my ministry had affected not only my own congregation, but was having repercussions on a much wider scale. I had to change my ways and, therefore, he had a proposition for me. Apparently, since all the persecution that I had received so far had not deterred me, they had decided to change gears and offer me an olive branch.

A pastor in the Circuit had been giving me a particularly rough time, and this judge offered to send some thugs to that pastor's home to assault him as a gesture of goodwill to me if I would be prepared to partner with them and possibly tone down my views of apartheid. If I did, he made it clear that I would receive several more "perks" from them besides the poor pastor being beaten up as a threat to him to back off.

The Lord had already showed me in my spirit that this pastor he was referring to was a pawn to this organization, and they obviously thought nothing of hurting one of their own for the sake of the greater cause. Every time I looked at that pastor after this meeting with the judge, I felt a pain in my heart knowing that he was so faithful to serve their cause and yet his faithfulness was not reciprocated by his brothers in this organization. His brothers were using him, and he was too blind to see it. It is also possible that the judge was wearing a wire, hoping he could get me to agree to something that would give them leverage to "control" me.

I looked at that judge in quiet disbelief and with all the courage and calmness that I could muster, I told him that I wasn't interested in his "gesture of goodwill," that God was my judge and God alone had my allegiance, and that I would never stoop so low as to have another human being assaulted. I walked away with every muscle in me as taught as steel, wondering if I was going to make it safely back to my car, reminding myself of Jeremiah 1:17 with every step.

A few months later, that same judge died of an aggressive cancer! During that same time, some leaders in my congregation and community also just suddenly dropped dead from heart attacks with no warning. I'm not God, and I can't judge, and I certainly can't say that their deaths had anything to do with my ministry; but it surely got my attention, and I knew, based on Jeremiah 1:17, that I could not afford to disobey God. Don't mess with "The Lord"!

I represent I AM WHO I AM. Who do you represent?

"For this is contained in Scripture: 'Behold, I lay in Zion a choice stone, a precious corner stone, and he who believes in Him will not be disappointed.' This precious value, then, is for you who believe; but for those who disbelieve, 'The stone which the builders rejected, this became the very corner stone', and, 'a stone of stumbling and a rock of offense'; for they stumble because they are disobedient to the word, and to this doom they were also appointed. But you [who are seated in Christ] are a chosen race, a royal priesthood, a holy nation, a people for God's own possession, so that you may proclaim the excellencies of Him who has called you out of darkness into His marvelous light; for you once were not a people, but now you are the people of God; you had not received mercy, but now you have received mercy." – 1 Peter 2:6-10

CHAPTER 7

Home Is Where The Heart Is

"Then Moses departed and returned to Jethro his father-in-law and said to him, 'Please, let me go, that I may return to my brethren who are in Egypt, and see if they are still alive.' And Jethro said to Moses, 'Go in peace.' Now the Lord said to Moses in Midian, 'Go back to Egypt, for all the men who were seeking your life are dead.' So Moses took his wife and his sons and mounted them on a donkey, and returned to the land of Egypt." – Exodus 4:18-20

It is often said that "home is where the heart is." As I read the above verses, I wondered where Moses' heart was as he travelled back to Egypt. When he first left Egypt, he was single, leaving his childhood home for the first time. Now, as he approached Egypt once again, he was married with responsibilities and a home life far different from the one he left behind in Egypt. Was he going home to Egypt to his Hebrew family, or was he leaving home—which would be Midian and Jethro's family? And what about the princess and the palace family? I wondered whether he had ever really been home in the true sense of the word, being the sojourner that he believed himself to be (Exodus 2:22).

While thinking about this, it led me to the question, "Where is a sojourner's home?" To me, this is an important question to ask, because, as Christians, just like Moses, we are sojourners on this earth (1 Peter 2:11). I came to the following conclusion: "Home really is where the heart is, and our hearts are supposed to be in Christ, therefore home is Christ."

My own walk with Christ has confirmed to me that home is not that building we leave in the morning and come back to in the evening; it's not family, it's not the town in which we live or the country or the culture or the nationality to which we belong; these things and people are blessings or curses, depending on how we relate to them. No, home for a Christian is *"Me in Christ and His Word in me"* (John 15:7).

Home is dynamic, supernatural, immortal and free, a Redeemer who never slumbers or sleeps (Psalm 121:4). Home is the unmovable Rock that cannot be shaken (Isaiah 26:4, Hebrews 12:28). Home is Peace, Safety and Tranquility Himself (Luke 2:14). Without Christ, there is no home. The Christ way of being Home is living in and from the presence of God, in and from that place in Christ that John talks about and this "being home in Christ" should be tangibly illustrated and demonstrated as a relational lifestyle through the living Christ church (Ephesians 2:19-22), the family of God.

Moses wasn't going home, and he wasn't leaving home. Moses was Home. He was in God, and God was in him. He was a type of living Christ church of his time, and many would find solace within his walls and ultimately experience Home, which was God Himself.

God paves the way for Moses.

Is there not your brother Aaron the Levite? . . . he is coming out to meet you; when he sees you, he will be glad in his heart . . . So he went and met him at the mountain of God and kissed him . . . Then Moses and Aaron went and assembled all the elders of the sons of Israel . . . So the people believed; and when they heard that the Lord was concerned about the sons of Israel and that He had seen their affliction then they bowed low and worshiped." – Exodus 4:14, 29

The idea of going back to Egypt on a very difficult assignment from God was daunting to Moses according to Exodus 4:1-17. How would people react to his return? After all, he didn't leave under the best of circumstances. The Pharaoh who wanted him dead was himself dead and buried, but what about the rest of the monarchy with whom he grew up? How would they react to Moses, the "traitor" prince, returning to Egypt? Who was currently on the throne? Was it somebody with whom he grew up? Was it somebody who held a grudge against him? How would they react to him once again pleading the plight of the Hebrew slaves, only this time openly under the umbrella of the Hebrew God, and therefore publicly forsaking his Egyptian roots?

And then there were the Hebrew slaves. In the past, they hadn't exactly cherished his presence either. Would a remnant of that past generation still be around to make his life difficult? Would the new generation of Hebrews be more receptive? What about his own Hebrew family? We assume he had lost contact with them. Did they feel abandoned by him? Did they harbor ill feelings towards him? Would they embrace him or reject him? Would they accept the fact that he was sent from God to deliver them from slavery and lead them as a nation to a new land filled with milk and honey and promises of blessing and abundance and freedom and independence?

God knew how daunting this return to Egypt was for Moses, and so He did a very sweet thing. He made Moses' initial contact with his brother and with the elders of Israel and the rest of the Hebrews a pleasant one. Behind the scenes, God personally met with Aaron and sent him to go out and meet Moses with a kiss, and He made Aaron's heart glad to see his brother (Exodus 4:14, 27). Moses got a hearty welcome from his brother and was escorted gladly to the elders of Israel after Moses shared God's assignment with Aaron (Exodus 4:28). When the elders heard Moses' story, they wholeheartedly embraced him, and the entire Hebrew nation worshiped God, thanking Him for intervening in their plight (Exodus 4:31). Ree! Markable!

God breaks the ice softly and sweetly with an anointing of favor that paves the way for Moses to gain access into the hearts of an entire nation called Israel. This type of favor from God is still available today to those who will persistently and consistently make God and His Word their home (Proverbs 3:1-4).

God's anointing of favor affects people's minds and hearts.

*"Go and gather the elders of Israel together and say to them . . . **They will pay heed to what you say** . . . And moreover, behold, he [Aaron] is coming out to meet you; when he sees you, **he will be glad in his heart.**"* – Exodus 3:16, 18; 4:14

Aaron and the elders of Israel in the above verses are just some of the many examples in the Bible of God giving an individual favor and thus supernaturally affecting peoples' hearts and minds favorably towards that individual and their cause. I witnessed this several times during my ministry as a pastor in South Africa.

One of those times was when I applied for the position of pastor in a Dutch Reformed congregation in South Africa. I was already relieving in the congregation as an interim pastor since they had lost their pastor to misconduct, but my application still caused shock waves through the congregation. They were willing to use me as an interim pastor because I was available, but, "The nerve of a woman to apply for the actual position of pastor!" was the general thought process.

Several men applied for the position; then, every applicant, including me, was given a Sunday to lead the service and preach. The church board, which consisted of twenty deacons and twenty elders, had the opportunity to interview each applicant after the service. After all the applicants received a turn to preach and go through their interview, the church board had to vote on each individual; the plan was to bring the top five back for round two. Shockingly I was in the top five.

The four other candidates were great, and . . . they were married, while I was not. The vibe on the street was that this congregation could not afford to have a single pastor, let alone a woman. They needed a man, and they needed his wife to lead the women's ministry. It was common knowledge that the congregations got two people for the price of one. The general consensus was that I was just all wrong for the position, and a message was sent by word of mouth to the board members that I could absolutely not be voted in again. Round two went very well, and the board once again had to vote so that they could pick the top three for round three. A gasp went through the congregation when the top three were announced, and I was one of them. "What's wrong with the board?" some people snarled in dismay. "Have they lost their minds?"

This was a farming community with an old-fashioned phone exchange, and the phone lines were buzzing. I found out later that the lady who worked at the exchange, through which all the calls were routed, couldn't help but giggle at all the choice words being used. She actually liked me and was secretly rooting for me. She was quite entertained by the flood of disapproval flowing through the lines. One thing was certain: the congregation was severely torn over a certain young lady, and that would be me. My application really upset the apple cart.

Round three was over, and once again the board had to vote—this time for "THE ONE." The word on the street was that they had been thoroughly threatened by so-called important congregation members and prominent community leaders alike. No woman and no single person could be a pastor in this congregation. Double whammy! The message was loud and clear. However, their worst nightmare came true when the ballots were counted and a certain young lady received over 70 percent of the votes.

It had to have been a supernatural intervention because, in the natural, it was considered impossible. The majority of the board members acknowledged later to their congregational constituents that they went in to vote with the full intention of not voting for me, and yet, when the ballots were counted, the board had voted me in as their pastor. When their congregational constituents demanded answers, they couldn't explain it.

I can. It's called the anointing of favor from God, and that anointing changed the hearts and minds of the majority of the board. When they took up their pens to vote, Holy Spirit came upon them, and they were moved to vote for me just like Aaron and the elders of Israel were moved to embrace Moses and his message from God.

Dear one, don't become so engrossed and entrenched in your circumstances and the landscape that surrounds you that you miss what God is doing. All is not as it seems. God is at work. Do your part as He leads you, and trust Him for His perfect outcome, which may or may not be what you expect but will be good, which in turn will ultimately be good for you and your influence circle. *"And we know that all things work together for good to those who love God, to those who are called according to His purposes"* – Romans 8:28.

Many years later, after resigning from the Dutch Reformed Church and working through all the hurt and pain and rejection I felt, I would come to realize that God orchestrated a Divine appointment with that congregation and me, and especially some of its leaders and surrounding leaders. I was His instrument. What God did through me, I realized later, He could only have done through a woman in that particular congregation.

At the time, however, neither the board nor the congregation nor I had any idea that we had been set up by God for a visitation from Him. God was also setting up Moses and Aaron and the Hebrew slaves and Pharaoh and the Egyptians for a visitation from Him.

Yes, God sets us up for His visitations.
"Thus says the Lord, the God of Israel, 'Let My people go that they may celebrate a feast to Me in the wilderness.'" – Exodus 5:1

By putting out the above request, God was setting the stage for a confrontation with the mighty Pharaoh of Egypt. During this confrontation, Pharaoh would come to realize that he was not the immortal god that he was raised to believe he was. At this point in time, Pharaoh was probably the most powerful leader in the known world, and he believed that he was the reincarnation and representative of the main Egyptian god, Ra. In his mind, there was no human more powerful than he and no god more powerful than the one he represented. God was about to shatter his world and religious view. Little did I or my congregation know that God was about to confront our world and religious views as well.

Enter setup

Sheila, who had specially relocated with me to continue serving me, knocked on my study door one day to inform me that I had a visitor. It was the pastor of the Black Dutch Reformed Church. We both pastored Dutch Reformed congregations, but served different communities. I pastored in the White part of town, he pastored in the Black part of town, and then there was also the Colored or Brown part of town. Each group had its own separate Dutch Reformed congregation.

Before I met this Black pastor, I didn't really give these distinctions much thought. It had been that way forever, and even though I didn't care for the animosity between the different groups, I concentrated on my White "flock" which, on the best of days, was a huge task.

This pastor was a tall, strong, humble Black man; and for some reason, I felt an immediate kinship with him. I intuitively felt that we were of the same Spirit, the Holy Spirit. At that point, the fact that he was Black and sitting on one of my chairs in my study didn't even create a bleep on my radar, even though White people generally did not allow Black people to sit on their furniture. To me, he was a human being and a brother in Christ, and that's all that mattered. For the next hour, he unfolded his story.

I had been with this congregation for only a few months at that point, and I had not yet taken the time to visit the other two Dutch Reformed congregations. The pastor started describing the poverty and the alcohol and drug abuse of the people in the Black congregation. As I listened intently, my thoughts went back to my hometown where Black people and poverty and alcohol just seemed to gravitate to each other. It just seemed a fact of life growing up—a distant fact of life. For the first time, it was represented to me as a reality, not just a distant knowledge. Apartheid had insulated me from all of this while I was growing up.

In front of me was a man who hadn't been paid in months, whose car was on its last legs, who was doing "piece" jobs (part-time work) to try to keep food on his table—his congregation unable to meet their commitments towards him. Our church did help some. As this man described the condition of his people and the broken down, crumbling condition of the church building in which they met, I felt his heart. He really cared for his "flock." Actually, I was waiting for him to ask for money for himself and his congregation, but that wasn't why he had come.

He came for the sake of his daughter who was exceptionally gifted. With the abolishment of apartheid, the White school had recently become a multi-racial school, causing about 90 percent of the Whites to send their children to private boarding schools instead. The White school (now multi-racial) had informed him that they could no longer accommodate his daughter's educational needs; she needed to go to a special school for gifted children, which was of course expensive. He asked if it were at all possible that the White congregation could help pay her tuition.

He looked so uncomfortable and vulnerable. I thought about my own struggles trying to make ends meet while getting through university. I had tasted small periods of not having money to buy food, of standing next to a car on the highway wondering how I was going to get the car home because I didn't have money for a tow truck. The Lord had always provided Good Samaritans, and as I looked at this vulnerable father in front of me, I thanked God for giving me a turn to be the Good Samaritan. "Of course the White congregation should help," I exclaimed. To me, this was a no-brainer!

I eagerly presented his need before the board at the next board meeting, thinking nothing of the fact that he was Black and we were White. It never occurred to me that it would be a problem or set off a series of events that would ultimately lead to a great divide in the congregation and eventually to my resignation from the Dutch Reformed Church. However, it would also confront White, Black and Brown people with the true gospel of Jesus Christ and ultimately force people to reassess their position in Christ.

God orchestrates events in order to fight for the souls of individuals and nations.

"There is no one like You among the gods, O Lord, nor are there any works like Yours. All nations whom You have made shall come and worship before You, O Lord, and they shall glorify Your name. For You are great and do wondrous deeds; You alone are God." – Psalm 86:8-10

God orchestrated events against Pharaoh and Egypt and Israel in order to fight for the souls of individuals, as well as the two nations as a whole. God orchestrated events in my South African congregation and the surrounding communities in order to fight for the souls of those people and, especially in my world, the souls of a White Afrikaner group of people. In both Egypt and my community, the events unfolded publicly, thereby confronting all participants and bystanders with Jesus Christ, challenging the true allegiance of their hearts.

Somewhere in the history of this White Dutch Reformed congregation, the majority of the members had made a paradigm shift. Their mindset moved from putting their faith in the Lord to putting their faith in an ideology. Somehow they started majoring in a faith in apartheid and their "Afrikanership," which ultimately and subtly led them to forsaking their first love, Jesus Christ. It seemed to me that somewhere in the history of this congregation, they had started building their spiritual foundation on proverbial sand called apartheid; and now that apartheid was abolished, the ground was shaking beneath them.

They were watching their beloved ideology's foundation crumble, and the "White Afrikaner kingdom" that they had built on that foundation was toppling over . . . and they were terrified. The majority of this congregation was riddled with fear, with only a few souls left who still had purity of faith in Christ; and these were being mercilessly persecuted by the rest. Never before and never since have I seen such a concentration of fear in one spot, and this fear manifested itself in all forms of anger, bitterness, hatred, lack of compassion, pride and even violence.

I learned during this time that fear and faith are two sides of the same coin, and that if we wanted to walk in faith, we had to learn to conquer fear—or at least learn to exercise faith in spite of our fear. Moses and Israel had to learn this. Pharaoh and Egypt had to learn this. I and my little congregation had to learn this.

Only when we embrace the true and living God and walk in faith in spite of our fear do we get to worship God on the mountain and live from that place in Christ that John talks about. Only when we lay down our lives for Him does He exalt our lives and lead us to great heights of influence and victory while we represent His kingdom and righteousness in our influence circles. Matthew writes in chapter 6, verse 24, *"No one can serve two masters; for either he will hate the one and love the other, or he will be devoted to one and despise the other. You cannot serve God and Mammon."* To put it in modern terms, you cannot serve God and your own selfish economic interests at the same time.

John 12:25 summarizes it well, *"He who loves his life loses it, and he who hates his life in this world will keep it to life eternal."* If you choose God, then God Himself will honor and preserve and prosper your life and the things and people you hold dear. If you choose your life, then you will have to depend on your own wits to defend it, which will limit you to your own strength and abilities and ultimately lead to your destruction, because there's always somebody or something stronger than you are.

I believe God sets up all of us through a series of events, so that every person and nation is at some point confronted with this truth and ultimately challenged to make the "God" choice. He draws the proverbial line in the sand, and those who make the "God" choice in spite of their fears get promoted to greater heights in Him and greater influence in society and in the world. Those who cling to their fears and refuse to make the shift are forced to live with the destructiveness of their own fear and the consequences of a dog-eat-dog world mindset.

God is fighting for the souls of individuals and nations, and He will send a Moses to confront your Pharaoh, whatever it is that Pharaoh represents in your life or a nation's life. Whatever you exalt above God will be tested and exposed for the "sand" that it is—not to embarrass or destroy you, but to hopefully bring you to God himself. Your soul or the soul of a nation is His priority, and only after that comes your mission or influence in society or in the world as a nation.

You are only truly home when your heart and your identity are in Him; only then can you provide a true, unshakeable home for others. Only then can you powerfully and permanently shape and influence a culture and a nation with kingdom principles. God will not entrust kingdom authority to a people who cling to fear and selfish economic ambitions. Ultimately, I believe, there will be a generation of kingdom children who will establish His kingdom and His righteousness on this earth. Entire nations will embrace Him and His kingdom culture because of this generation. Matthew 28:19 tells us, *"Go therefore and make disciples of all the nations . . . "* Notice, Matthew doesn't refer to individuals inside nations becoming disciples; he refers to entire nations becoming disciples. God has nations in His crosshairs.

God is setting us up, sifting us, purifying us for the sake of our souls and ultimately for the souls of entire nations. Pharaoh represented an entire nation, Moses represented an entire nation, and God set them up through a series of events in order to challenge them to set their fears and warped mindsets aside and become kingdom nations. Pharaoh failed, Moses buckled, but God's dream lived on and still lives on in the hearts and minds of modern Joshuas and Calebs and Daniels and Davids and Solomons and Elijahs and Pauls and Peters and Johns and . . . (can you put your name in here?). He is raising them up in this end time to collectively become a kingdom generation through the outpouring of His Spirit in the name of Jesus (Acts 2:17-21). Collectively they will become living demonstrations and testimonies of His great and wonderful works, which will ultimately cause the "Queens of Sheba" (1 Kings 10) of this earth and their nations to bow before Him and acknowledge that He is God. The line is being drawn, and the challenge is being made. Will you become a catalyst that challenges nations and their leaders to honor and embrace Him and His kingdom culture? Will you abandon your Mammon and recklessly, lavishly love and follow Christ, no matter the cost?

God sent me as a type of Moses to challenge a small White Dutch Reformed congregation to abandon their Mammon called apartheid in exchange for Him and His kingdom. The irony of the situation is, they were also a type of Moses sent to challenge me to abandon my Mammon called the pulpit in exchange for Him and His kingdom. Our hour of visitation had come, and so also for Pharaoh and Moses and Egypt and Israel.

"And it will be in the last days, God says, that I will pour forth of My Spirit on all mankind; and your sons and your daughters shall prophesy and your young men shall see visions, and your old men shall dream dreams; even on my bondslaves, both men and women, I will in those days pour forth of My Spirit and they shall prophesy." – Acts 2:17-18

CHAPTER 8

The Fear of God Versus The Fear of Man

"The fear of the Lord is the beginning of wisdom." – Proverbs 9:10

When I left the river after my encounter with the judge, I left with a certain amount of fear in my heart and understood why God had highlighted Jeremiah 1:17 in my quiet time before the incident: *"Do not be dismayed before them, or I will dismay you before them."* God had prepared me to face my fear and make the right choice. By God's grace, I had learned to fear God more than I feared the judge in that moment of interaction with him. In fact, I was so sold out to God, so totally in love with God, I was unable to grasp or even entertain what the judge was offering me. You see, the fear of God and the love of God are inseparable.

As I walked away, numb and shocked, I knew that even if I lost everything in the process, I would retain my soul and my relationship with my

Redeemer; and that's all that mattered. Little did I know that my resolve would be tested and retested in the months that followed and that I would eventually have to make the ultimate choice—my career or God.

A theophany and Moses' commission

"God called to him from the midst of the bush and said, 'Moses, Moses . . . I will send you to Pharaoh, so that you may bring My people, the sons of Israel, out of Egypt.'" – Exodus 3:4, 10

I've already mentioned this, but it's worth repeating. Every individual in the Bible who received a Divine assignment got it through some kind of theophany. If you're wondering what a theophany is, simply stated, it is a manifestation of God that is tangible to the human senses. The appearance of the Angel of the Lord is also often looked upon as a theophany, as this angel is often interpreted as the pre-incarnate Christ.

The entire Bible is full of these experiences. I encourage you to read the stories of Abraham, Jacob, Aaron, Joshua, Solomon, David, Daniel and his friends, the disciples, Saul who became Paul, and many more to see how God entered their private space in a tangible fashion to commission and re-commission them throughout their lives. God came to these people through burning bushes (signs and wonders), dreams, visions, Holy Spirit baptisms, an audible voice, messengers called angels, etc. Most of these individuals understood not only the love of God, but also the fear of God. Being visited by the living God of the universe is both wonderful and scary at the same time. If a visitation from the living God doesn't fill you with awe and fear and respect and make you tremble at the knees, then nothing will. In addition, the commissions that came with these visitations were truly frightening assignments for mere human beings, and sometimes the motivation to obey God and tackle these assignments had to initially come from their fear of God and the consequences of disobedience rather than their love for God.

Most of these individuals loved God with all their heart or they learned to over time, because He is a gracious and loving God; but when you are still a greenhorn in your relationship with God and the commission makes your knees weak and your blood run cold, you need the fear of God as well to make it to the other side. Let me put it this way. There are moments when denying a commission is like selling your soul, and it would behoove anybody in that position to remember the consequences of selling their soul. God is our Father, one thousand times yes, but He is also our judge.

The church today all too often concentrates on the "Sugar Daddy" image of God and neglects the "Righteous Judge". The love of God is real, and His overwhelming grace and mercy should be celebrated and embraced; but dare I say the love of God has often been watered down to a "tickle my flesh," "pally-pally," high five, and the church has almost completely lost the fear of God. I find it interesting that Proverbs 9:10 says that the *"fear of the Lord is the beginning of wisdom."* The fear of the Lord is apparently, according to Proverbs, a component of the foundation upon which wisdom is built, and wisdom leads to knowledge and understanding, which leads to revelation, which leads to vision; and the Bible says that God's people perish for a lack of vision (Proverbs 29:18). Could it be that people are perishing and the church is losing her influence in society because we essentially lack one of the essential building blocks of wisdom called *"the fear of the Lord"*?

You see, *"the fear of the Lord"* creates restraints in peoples' lives by turning hearts to God's ways, putting them on a specific road that is clearly marked by Him. As people progress on this road, while being obedient to the markings or restraints, they attract more of God into their lives; and as they attract more of Him, they receive more revelation (Divine guidance) from Him. The more revelation they receive, the clearer the road becomes, and the freer they actually become in and through Him. The restraints actually promote freedom.

Proverbs 29:18 (NLT) says that, *"When people do not accept divine guidance, they run wild."* The NASB says people become "unrestrained."

Somebody once made the statement to me that he thought this world had gone mad. He was referring to things he was seeing on the news about the views and behavior of society in general, but also experiences he was having with church people on a day-to-day basis. I want to submit that the root of the madness he is observing is a lack of the fear of the Lord. When the masses cast away the fear of God, anything goes.

Proverbs 29:18 also states that those who obey these restraints are blessed. Some translations state that those who obey are filled with joy and happiness. They are still faced with the assignment and the restraints, but because of their obedience, God goes with them and supplies all the tools they need. Eventually the joy of the Lord becomes their strength by surpassing the fear of the Lord. Eventually, the restraints are thrown off, like training wheels are removed from a bicycle, because we have become one with the living God and His heart and His mind. It's then that we get to ask whatever we wish and it will be given according to John 15:7; it's not to run wild, but to flow with and from the heart and mind of God.

Moses discovered what it was like to have the training wheels removed. God equipped Moses with a mouthpiece called Aaron, a staff that gave him the ability to perform signs and wonders, a huge measure of Holy Spirit anointing, favor with the elders, and most importantly, God's own presence. Moses and the Israelites through him were able to live a supernatural life in the natural world with the presence of God in their midst. Now that is something to be joyful and happy about!

This supernatural life was birthed, though, within the parameters of constraints set by the fear of the Lord. The love of the Lord and the fear of the Lord are inseparable. Majoring on one while neglecting the other leads to a carnal theology.

"'In an outburst of anger I hid My face from you for a moment, but with everlasting loving-kindness I will have compassion on you,' says the Lord your Redeemer" (Isaiah 54:8). I've chosen this verse just to illustrate that God clearly has two sides, and we had better acknowledge both. Dare I say that we can't even begin to understand the love of God if we don't have

a healthy fear of God? I'm emphasizing the term "healthy" here because healthy fear leads us *to* God, *to* his Heart. Healthy fear causes us to weigh every action, every thought, every decision against the backdrop of God's heart and His restraints; it causes us to choose God every time, which in turn brings more and more of God and His favor and love into our lives until we find ourselves fully in love with God. The more mature we become in our relationship with the Lord, the more we major on love instead of fear.

There is no liberty amongst people groups, however, without the fear of God. Without the fear of God, there is only increasing anarchy—people running wild—because without the fear of God, evil abounds and love waxes cold.

The moment of truth—the choice between man and God

"The foremen of the sons of Israel were beaten . . . The foremen of the sons of Israel saw that they were in trouble . . . they met Moses and Aaron . . . They said to them, 'May the Lord look upon you and judge you, for you have made us odious in Pharaoh's sight and in the sight of his servants, to put a sword in their hand to kill us.'" – Exodus 5:14, 19-21

"Ever since I came to Pharaoh to speak in Your name, he has done harm to this people, and You have not delivered Your people at all." – Exodus 5:23

God's calling on an individual's life has repercussions. Every assignment comes with a cost, and that cost doesn't just affect the individual who has the calling; it affects everybody around that individual. God's calling, God's ways put an initial squeeze on people and their surroundings; and when people are squeezed, they often become intoxicated with emotions. Pain is emotional and blinding, and many assignments from God have been abandoned at the crossroads of a painful, sobering squeeze, when reality suddenly sets in, and the cost to follow God into that place of assignment becomes apparent and emotionally overwhelming. It's the moment of truth . . . will you still follow God in the midst of aggressive and sometimes even dangerous resistance?

Pharaoh was the most powerful king in the time of Moses and Israel, and Egypt was the most powerful kingdom. You certainly did not want to get on the wrong side of Pharaoh. Israel was owned by Pharaoh as a nation of slaves to do whatever Pharaoh commanded them to do. Moses was a "nobody" in the eyes of Pharaoh and Israel. He renounced his right to be a prince in the Egyptian palace the day he killed an Egyptian soldier as an act of solidarity with Israel. That's how Mr. Nobody found himself in a position where Israel did not appreciate his act of solidarity at all, the Pharaoh wanted to kill him, and he ended up far away in the obliviousness of a desert taking care of his father-in-law's sheep for forty years, completely removed from Israel and Egypt and the monarchy and the whole issue of Hebrew slavery to which he seemed drawn.

Initially, for a short time after the return of Mr. Nobody, Israel embraced Moses and his wonderful tale of having a visitation from God and coming as their liberator in the name of the Lord (Exodus 3:15). They *"believed"* Moses and *"bowed low and worshipped God"* (Exodus 4:31). They were so ready to be liberated, so ready to follow God and Moses . . . or were they? Did they honestly think that Pharaoh was just going to sit back and allow them to leave? Or maybe they thought God would just zap Pharaoh unconscious or dead? Apparently they never considered the possibility that following God and Moses out of Egypt to their freedom would entail resistance from Pharaoh and his dark forces. Suddenly they didn't "believe" in God's plan of liberation for them anymore. Their faith succumbed to their fear of Pharaoh.

In their defense, they did not know the God of their forefathers very well, and they had no confidence in Mr. Nobody. All they knew for sure was the tyranny of which Pharaoh was capable. Notice the difference in response to the tyranny of Pharaoh between Israel and Moses. The

Israelites reacted to Pharaoh and his tyranny by threatening Moses with grave consequences for his actions. They wanted nothing more to do with Moses and his so-called revelation from God. They just wanted to go back to their slavery, try to keep the peace and hopefully iron things out with the Pharaoh, and definitely forget about God and freedom. Moses, on the other hand, reacted to Pharaoh and his tyranny by running straight to God.

Israel feared Pharaoh and immediately cowered before him and abandoned God; Moses feared God and immediately stormed the throne room of heaven, putting a demand on God and His promise of deliverance. Just to be clear here, though, both were wailing and complaining—Moses just happened to go to the right Source. Moses still had some trust issues himself, but at least he was on his way to partnering with this supernatural God. Israel was heading entirely in the opposite direction toward resentment and distrust and the wrong kind of fear; and it showed in their behavior.

Just so you know, whether you choose God or man, there is a cost.

"'I will bring you to the land which I swore to give to Abraham, Isaac, and Jacob, and I will give it to you for a possession; I am the Lord.' So Moses spoke thus to the sons of Israel, but they did not listen to Moses on account of their despondency and cruel bondage." – Exodus 6:9-10

While driving back to the town where I pastored, back to my little congregation, after my meeting with the judge at the river, my thoughts were in turmoil. I still found it hard to digest that a prominent man of the law like a judge would actually offer to send thugs to a pastor's house and have him assaulted just to gain my co-operation and to let the pastor know that he should back off. With whom exactly was I dealing? It's true that the pastor was persecuting me because of my stance against segregation in the church and was making it his business to cause resistance against me, but to send thugs to assault him was just beyond my comprehension. The judge also mentioned that if I would cooperate, I would receive many favors and the added bonus of this organization's protection. I had absolutely no desire to receive any favors from the likes of him or his organization, but what was alarming to me was the underlying threat or consequences that would follow if I did not cooperate. I wondered just how far these people would go to protect their beloved apartheid. What exactly did I need protection from? Could the persecution possibly get any worse? I would soon find out . . .

The Hebrew slaves were reeling under the new work load requirements from Pharaoh, and they were being mercilessly flogged by Pharaoh's soldiers for not being able to comply with them. How terrible Moses must have felt for the suffering of his fellow Hebrews, especially when he thought about their suffering increasing because of him . . . actually, because of God and him. The fact that God had warned him beforehand that Pharaoh would reject God's request and that it would take force to leave Egypt had totally eluded him (Exodus 3:19). Moses knew what it meant to suffer personally for the cause of God, but to watch others suffer and to know that he had played a part in their suffering was too much for Moses to bear; he broke down before God (Exodus 5:23; 6:12).

When I got back to the parsonage, life started getting a whole lot harder. I never did speak to or see the judge again, but he and those in his organization had very clearly declared war. It would affect my most faithful followers in such a profound way that it would break my heart and drive me to my knees constantly. I, too, wailed before God more times than I care to remember. I don't remember the words I prayed anymore, but I do still remember the pain and heaviness of the knowledge that people were suffering persecution because of a cause I was leading for the sake of Christ. However, those same people assured me that they would not have it any other way. To them, it was Christ or nothing; and Christ died for Black and Colored people too.

The cost of choosing man

After congregation members filed an article 12 against me, the Circuit pastors insisted that I visit every disgruntled member in the church and try to reason with them and make peace. I was sitting in the living room of one of my deacons one day, a young married man with children who owned a big sheep and cattle ranch. He and I debated the whole issue of apartheid as pertaining to the church. Was it really biblical to deny people access to a church of Christ based on the color of their skin? We were heavy in discussion when I suddenly saw a light bulb go off in his head. I knew Holy Spirit was revealing truth to him. He was being convicted, and for a moment I had hope that this man would change his stance. I could see that he really wanted to as, right before my eyes, tears started trickling down his face. It was clear he now understood the heart of Christ; but he was so deep in debt to the likes of the judge and the organization he represented that he could not turn back. I soon realized they were tears of sorrow, because he was so entwined in an evil web that he did not have the courage to stand up to it. His fear of "Pharaoh" was greater than the knowledge of Christ that had just pierced his heart. He was trapped. He feared "Pharaoh" more than he feared God.

One day I was driving on a remote road when a farmer waved me down with his vehicle. At first I was afraid, because it was hard for me at that point to discern between friend and foe. However, I could not ignore the man. I had a revolver under my seat, but I realized that I couldn't get out of my truck with the revolver; that just wouldn't look right. So, I tried to devise a plan in my head to get it if I needed it. Once I got out of the truck, I aborted the idea, knowing that I would never make it back to my truck in time. I was vulnerable and just had to trust God to protect me.

Thankfully, he was a friend, and he wanted to talk to me in a private place, which was on the side of a road in the middle of nowhere. He did not want the "powers that be" to know that he had made contact with me, because as he unfolded his story, it became clear that he and his family would suffer dire consequences. Come to find out, the organization represented by the judge literally owned this part of the world, because they knew how to manipulate the farmers' livelihoods. They owned the agents who worked as middlemen between the farmers and the market, and if the farmers didn't adhere to their rules and their bribes, then their livestock was denied access to the market, causing economic devastation to the farmer and his family.

Over the years, these unscrupulous men had also done favors for some of these farmers which sucked them deeper and deeper into an indebted web from which there was seemingly no escape, except at great cost. Some of these farmers were actual members of the organization, and others had been enslaved into being their pawns. Either way, they were compelled to conform to a code of conduct enforced by this organization or else bear the consequences. He told me about farmers who had lost everything because they refused to conform. According to him, this organization had made examples of some farmers so that the rest wouldn't dare to stand up against them.

He wanted me to know what kind of underground force I was fighting, but he also wanted to encourage me to keep up the good fight. He said he had a high degree of respect for me, and that he was rooting for me from the shadows of his farm. (Hmm.) Somebody had to break this web, and he was hoping that that somebody would be me. Choosing man had enslaved a large part of this community to a manmade ideology and a ruthless secret body that governed that ideology.

I drove on, now fully understanding why my deacon had wept in his living room, and my heart felt oh so heavy. I cried for him and my congregation and for me and for the evil that was darkening the hearts of so many. "Why, Lord, did You choose me? I am so out of my league. What could I, a seemingly naïve young woman, possibly do to bring Your light to such a dark place?"

The cost of choosing God

"Why me, Lord?" As I meditated on that question, it came to me that every male pastor who had pastored my current congregation before me had been approached by this organization, if and when necessary, and was expected to conform to their rules or be driven out of town. They were a secret male organization used to working with and bribing and threatening males, but they had never before had to deal with a female as the pastor.

God threw them off kilter by sending a woman to resist them, giving me two years to preach the true Gospel to their faces, and therefore giving them the opportunity to repent from their crooked ways. God was fighting for their souls, and my gender kept them at bay long enough for Him to really get under their skin, like the deacon crying in his living room.

Towards the end of the second year, however, I realized that my gender would not protect me much longer. Their hatred was becoming brazen enough for some at least to become violent, even towards a woman. All of hell was breaking loose and descending on that little town. My foe was invisible and relentless and heartless, but I was still determined to stand for Christ's message of love for all people. As long as I pastored that church, those church doors would welcome everybody. But people were getting hurt . . .

I walked into a store one day that was owned by two of my most faithful elders, a husband and wife whom I respected and loved very much. They took me aside and told me that they had been warned by members of this organization that if they continued to support my efforts to fight against segregation in that congregation, their store would be boycotted and shut down. They had both worked until retirement in different fields and, once retired, put all their retirement money into their store, realizing a lifelong dream of owning their own business. They assured me, however, that they were not going to waiver in their stance. According to them, their love for and fear of God superseded any threat of this kind; but I could feel their pain and understood the weightiness of the consequences. I had already made up my mind that I would go under with this ship if I had to, but seeing others whom I loved go under too . . . that reality made me cringe.

At home, in the parsonage, I had a grandmother who was spiraling into a devastating depression and buckling under kidney and congestive heart failure. My own esophagus had gone into such a spasm that I could hardly swallow, and my colon was so inflamed and spastic that I could hardly stand up straight. I had also almost suffered a blackout or two from hypoglycemia and even broke a rib one morning getting up, because of muscles being so taught that they literally snapped the rib. Stress was taking its toll!

One night the phone rang, and it was a young boy crying and begging me to come to the ranch where he lived. He said his parents were having a terrible fight, and he was scared. I could hear them screaming in the background. It was very late, and I knew that the ranch was remote. I would have to drive in the pitch dark of the night on a lonely, winding dirt road to get there. The first thought that came to my mind was, "Is this authentic, or are 'they' using this boy to coax me out into the night in order to ambush me?"

My grandmother had heard the phone and was by this time standing by my side with question marks on her face. I told her briefly what the child had told me and told her not to wait up for me as I did not know how long it would take. She was instantly hysterical, vocalizing exactly what I was thinking. She was convinced that I was going to be killed or at the very least be roughed up and hurt. In that moment, I realized just how much of a price she was paying in order for me to continue my ministry. I left my hysterical grandmother behind and rode off into the night. Thankfully, the call was authentic, and I arrived back home safely.

My grandmother's congestive heart failure and kidney disease started deteriorating under the pressure. Sheila noticed it before I did. One morning, I found Sheila bathing my grandmother and helping her to dress. Sheila and I became caregivers over night. In the midst of all this, Sheila was also aging; and she too, unbeknownst to me, was deteriorating. Her struggles of being a widow with wayward children, having a grandchild born out of wedlock growing up with no parental guidance, her struggles of poverty in squatter camps, the hatred that came with racism, the pressures of a parsonage in the middle of a hate-filled society, was all taking its toll on her too.

Sheila also smoked heavily, and her lungs were packing up. And yet, she was determined to see me established. I wanted her to retire and just let me take care of her, but she was on a mission to take care of me. By this time her daughter, a single mom, and grandson were living in a squatter camp far away. Sheila's daughter was basically selling herself as a prostitute to make ends meet, and her son was running wild in the squatter camp. This brought Sheila great sorrow.

After a year, Sheila came into my study one morning with that serious look on her face. She told me she believed she had done what the Lord asked her to do. She said she felt like she had taken me as far as she could; her assignment had been to see me established as a pastor, and she felt she had done that. She said it was time for her to go and look for her grandson and try to keep him from becoming another gang statistic. She also told me that this place I was pastoring was not friendly; there was no love there. She felt that living with me was just a recipe for more heartache and pain.

I begged her to stay, knowing she wouldn't make it in a squatter's camp. Tin shacks, frigid cold in the winter, stifling heat in the summer, sharing one outside toilet and spicket with ten or twenty tin shacks overflowing with people. There was no way she, and elderly person with health issues, could survive. I could not change Sheila's mind though. She was determined to save her grandson. He was her next assignment.

I didn't have much money. I had student debt that would take me a lifetime to pay off. I was driving an old vintage Citroen at the time that was on its last legs. The only phone I had was the one in the parsonage, which was a party line. Sheila and I both knew we would never see each other again once she left. It was even more dangerous for me to go into the squatter camps than it was for her to live with me. I parted ways with Sheila with a very heavy heart. In the congregation and in my own personal life, segregation was tearing at the very core of my heart.

Sheila left in the summer. In the middle of the following winter, the exchange lady called and asked if I would receive a reverse charge call. When she told me who the caller was, I knew it was bad news. It was Sheila's daughter. Sheila had succumbed to an asthma attack. During winter in the squatter's camp, they burn primitive wood stoves inside the tin shacks which give off a lot of smoke; this isn't good for healthy lungs, let alone sick ones. They had no phones, almost nobody owned a vehicle, and the hospital was far away. There was no 911. The inevitable had happened.

Sheila gave her life in the name of love. In her humble, broken way, she demonstrated Jesus like nobody else I know. Her daughter was calling me because they didn't have money for her funeral. I didn't either, but I borrowed the money from the bank, and we buried Sheila. Looking back I realize, my grandmother in many ways, gave her life too in the name of love, serving me and a costly calling.

Choosing God is not for the fainthearted! It's the moment of truth . . . will you still follow God in the midst of aggressive and sometimes even dangerous resistance? What if that resistance threatens the people you love? Only the fear of the Lord, which takes refuge in His love and mercy, can answer that question (Proverbs 9:10, Jeremiah 1:17).

"Who is the man who fears the Lord? He will instruct him in the way he should choose. His soul will abide in prosperity, and his descendants will inherit the land. The secret of the Lord is for those who fear Him, And He will make them know His covenant. My eyes are continually toward the Lord, For He will pluck my feet out of the net. Turn to me and be gracious to me, For I am lonely and afflicted. The troubles of my heart are enlarged; Bring me out of my distress. Look upon my affliction and my trouble, and forgive all my sins. Look upon my enemies, for they are many, and they hate me with violent hatred. Guard my soul and deliver me; Do not let me be ashamed, for I take refuge in You. Let integrity and uprightness preserve me, For I wait for You. Redeem Israel, O God, Out of all his troubles." – Psalm 25:12-22

CHAPTER 9

The Exodus

"Then he called for Moses and Aaron at night and said, 'Rise up, get out from among my people, both you and the sons of Israel; and go, worship the Lord, as you have said.'" – Exodus 12:31

Something I envy about Moses and his relationship with God is the fact that God spoke clearly to him. *"Thus the Lord used to speak to Moses face to face, just as a man speaks to his friend"* (Exodus 33:11). I meditate on that verse often, believing that there will come a day when I, too, will have such an intimate relationship with the great I AM. I want to know Him, I want to feel His heartbeat for humanity, I want to be so one with Him that my entire being flows from His heart and His mind. God is not a respecter of persons. If He did it for Moses, He will do it for you and for me.

God also uses people to speak to us, though. In a very critical moment, God used Pharaoh to give Moses a command: "Moses, take your people and get out of Egypt, now! And as you go, please bless us so that no further ill befalls us, but do leave." *"And on that same day the Lord brought the sons of Israel out of the land of Egypt by their hosts"* (Exodus 12:51).

Imagine leaving a place, in haste I might add, that you and your ancestors had inhabited for four hundred years, to go to a place you had never seen, maybe never even heard of. And all you have as a compass is a prophet called Moses and a God that just shocked the entire world with His supernatural feats over Pharaoh in the form of ten plagues. You can read all about it in Exodus, chapters 7 through 12. "Who is this God?" Behind you is the only home you've ever known, and in front of you is a big unknown desert. Your innards warn you that you had better be sure that you heard right or else you're in for huge heartache and calamity. "Can this God and the man of God really be trusted?" Little ones, livestock, women, men, strangers, all following a dream of freedom and promise. "What have we done?" is a haunting question ringing in your ears, but there is no turning back. The time has come: "Get out of Egypt, now!"

The revelation from God is precise and clear
"Now the Lord said to Moses 'One more plague I will bring on Pharaoh and on Egypt; after that he will let you go from here.'" – Exodus 11:1

The Lord doesn't speak to me as clearly as He did to Moses. How about you? With me it's a process. Sometimes it's Scripture that jumps out at me. Other times, it's things that people say and/or circumstances that leave impressions on my mind that I can't shake. I also have dreams and sometimes even visions. The dreams and visions are always in "parable" form, so I have to wait for the Lord to interpret, which in itself is a process most of the time. Often it's a combination of all of the above.

Something that I've learned over the years is that, not only do I get to embrace revelation, but I have to learn to embrace and enjoy God's mysteries as well. Solomon actually talks about this in Proverbs 25:2 when he says, *"It is the glory of God to conceal a thing: but the glory of kings [God's children] is to search out a matter."* I've learned that God purposely hides some revelation, which is only revealed to those who go after it, who search it out until they find it and understand it; and even then, it sometimes comes in the softest whisper, so that if you're not listening very carefully, you can actually miss it. Some revelation is so special to God that He shares it only with the ones who display the most hunger for it. But that's a different book.

Let me get back on track with this one. Like I said, for me, hearing from God is a process; and slowly but surely through a process, the Lord started speaking to me about the fact that it was time to leave, not only the little congregation I was leading, but the Dutch Reformed Church as an entity. Eventually, He would lead me out of South Africa to a foreign country called America. So, the Lord started preparing my heart for this journey. At this point, I even had pastors calling me from other parts of the country, telling me how they respected the stance I was taking. They knew what was going on because it had been displayed all over the newspapers throughout the country. They encouraged me to keep standing, but at the same time told me they could never take the stance I was taking, because they were afraid they would lose their positions as pastors, and they had families to support. They said I did have their prayers though. I even got a phone call from a member high up in the synod. It reminded me of the farmer praying for me from the shadows of his farm. Hmmm . . .

Is something wrong with this picture, or am I the only one that has a problem with it? On the one hand, I had understanding for their plight, sort of . . . but I also had a rough time digesting the integrity of it. How do you profess and preach Jesus, but then when it comes down to the wire, forsake Him for the sake of your own life and interests?

I also had some very smug pastors of our Circuit—though not all of them, thankfully—pointing fingers at me and chastising me for causing division in the church. One of those pastors looked me in the eye at a Circuit meeting one day and told me that I needed to back off because, according to him, I had no idea what I was dealing with. We were in a discussion about this secret organization that had invaded my congregation's life. He was young and yet immaculately dressed in an expensive suit, and he drove a Mercedes Benz. I couldn't help but wonder . . . had he accepted their favors? I will never know on this side of heaven, but his remark did strike me as odd. What did he mean when he said I had no idea what I was dealing with?

The final "get out of Egypt" revelation happened to me in the midst of an appointment I had with one of my former theology professors at university. I had made an appointment with him because the Lord showed me that he played a key role in the apartheid debate. The Lord had also shown me that he was going to go up in the synod and possibly lead the Dutch Reformed Church in that province. I wanted to speak with him because I wanted to ascertain whether he was part of the judge's organization or the Lord's army. I walked out of his office with a resolute knowledge that he was part of the organization; I knew it was time to leave. Several years went by before I wrote this book and after I wrote it, it resided in my computer for almost four years before I started the final editing work to get it ready for publication. During that time, this professor did become the head of the synod and his true colors became evident. Recently he was forced to resign in disgrace because of infidelity.

Resigning from the Dutch Reformed Church was no small thing for me. I had spent nine long, hard years studying theology just to become qualified to minister in the Dutch Reformed Church. Then I had to wait another whole year before I actually got involved in this congregation, only to go through an excruciating vetting process which lasted almost another year before actually becoming their pastor. And that doesn't even take into account the persecution throughout the entire process, starting from day one when I walked out of the registration office at University after changing from medicine to theology. It took almost eleven years for me to become a pastor. Now, after only two years of stormy ministry, the Lord seemed to be asking me to leave. "Forgive me for doubting, Lord, but am I hearing You correctly? Maybe it's just judgmentalism or battle-fatigue making me want to leave? Maybe I just need an attitude adjustment. Is this really You, Lord?"

The Lord gave me several confirmations from Scripture and other avenues over the next several days. Yes, hearing from God is often a process, but once the final Word is spoken, things move rather quickly. I was meditating on Jeremiah 51 when verse 6 jumped out at me as a "now" revelation from the Lord to me about the Dutch Reformed Church. Holy Spirit quickened verse 6 in my spirit: *"Flee from the midst of Babylon, and each of you save his life! Do not be destroyed in her punishment, for this is the Lord's time of vengeance; He is going to render recompense to her."* This was God's way of telling me, "Get out of Egypt, now!"

Today the Dutch Reformed Church is just a shell of what she once was. Her influence as a church body has dwindled to a trickle. Dare I say that judgment upon her as a church body did come? And I don't take delight in writing that. My prayer is that the remnant will once again embrace God as their first love and be the true light of their world as they once again engage Christ and His agenda for mankind, this time without compromise. I pray that a new generation of Christ followers, irrespective of color, creed, language or denomination, will emerge in South Africa and all across the world, picking up their crosses and following Jesus (Matthew 16:24-26) in an authentic, refreshing, compelling way that will cause the world to acknowledge Jesus and throw down their idols of opinions and speculations and ideologies and run to the only One who has real solutions for real-time personal, national and international crises. The fear of God really is the beginning of wisdom, and the world desperately needs true wisdom, the kind that only God can give through a yielded follower! Will you, dear reader, answer Jesus' call and be that yielded follower?

I resigned from the Dutch Reformed Church towards the end of 1998, but the anguish and doubt and questions still haunted me for several years. Did I really hear God correctly? Was I really supposed to resign? It was only in November 2014, approximately sixteen years after I resigned, that God finally released a couple of revelations to me—one through Scripture during a quiet time, and the other through two visiting prophets to our church—that began to put these questions to rest in my soul, launching a process of closure in my heart and my mind.

God speaks through visiting prophets.

On Wednesday night, November 5, 2014, our church held a prophetic event with three visiting prophets, one of them actually coming from England. At the time, I was taking care of Doris and had not attended church in several years because of caring for Doris and Elwood around the clock. By this time, Elwood had passed away, and Doris was approaching the end of her life. I had not lost contact with our local church though, and when this event was announced; I felt a very strong prompting from Holy Spirit to attend.

I asked Doris' sister if she would mind staying with Doris that night so that I could go. I slipped in as the event started and sat down in the back row. I purposely chose to sit behind a tall man so that I would not be easily spotted. For some reason, I wanted to be unnoticed, knowing that prophets would be on the stage. I wanted to hide in case they singled me out like prophets sometimes do. I knew Holy Spirit was up to something, and I was a little nervous. I also had not been amongst people for a very long time, and I felt a little insecure with so many people around me.

The event started with praise and worship and, during worship, I suddenly saw lots and lots of fire come down from heaven in my mind's eye. It washed over me and through me, feeling soothing and wonderful; and for the first time in a long time, I felt joy flood my being. While this was going on, I saw Jesus in the fire with His arms stretched out to me; and I got sucked into and flew over heavenly realms, feeling much joy! This was all in a vision of course. When the worship ended, I sat down, refreshed, humbled and full of joy. He touched me profoundly!

The three prophets got up on the stage, and the prophet from England walked to the end of the stage, peered around the tall man in front of me, pointed at me and asked me to stand. I glanced around me and behind me, wondering if maybe he was pointing at someone else; but then he said, "You in the light blue shirt behind that gentleman, will you please stand, I have a word from the Lord for you." Did God have an appointment with me or what?

I wrote down what he said when I got home, and this is the gist of it. He told me that I had been very badly hurt by someone or some kind of entity in the past, and that he was led to represent that someone or entity and personally apologize to me on their behalf for the hurt. He said that I had been carrying guilt and shame and a sense of failure for far too long, that I had been beating myself up, and that it was time to stop. He then proceeded to apologize in the most heartfelt, heart-wrenching way for the abuse that I had suffered. His apology penetrated my brokenness and left me weeping profusely as he spoke.

He then went on to say that I had been interceding for people (family, friends and others) without seeing much fruit, but that was about to change. However, before I saw change, I would first go through a season of taking care of myself as I had been carrying other people's burdens and neglecting myself for far too long. God was first going to take me through a season of focusing on me. At the time, I had no idea that, after Doris's death, I would go through an intensely painful and rewarding season of healing and restoration.

After the first prophet was done, the next one came forward and started prophesying that there was someone in the audience that used to be in ministry but wasn't anymore. This somebody had walked away from ministry and was now struggling with a sense of guilt and shame, wondering if they had missed it and wondering if God would ever give them another chance. He said God wasn't done and that this person was at the event for a reason. God wanted the person to know that He was going to give them an opportunity to minister again.

I knew Holy Spirit was speaking to me. I had not attended church in several years, and it would be April 2016 before I would physically enter that church again after Doris' death. Holy Spirit led me there that night. He had a Divine appointment with me, and I left cleansed, refreshed and encouraged, thanking God for His presence, love and affirmation.

God speaks through dreams.

Towards the end of December 2014, I had a dream that I was in a building with a group of male theologians. They had invited a visiting professor to address the group, but there was a problem. He did not have a robe to wear and, as a speaker, he could not go on the stage without a robe. The group decided to "unrobe" me and have him wear my robe.

He ministered to us and then spent time visiting with us, wearing my robe the whole time. As he started to leave, I realized he was leaving with my robe. He seemed oblivious to the fact that it belonged to me. I followed him out and informed him that the robe was mine and that, while I had been more than happy to loan it to him for the event, I wanted it back since he was leaving.

He took off the robe and laid it on a nearby counter; to my horror, I noticed that he had cut off the roses a friend had sewn on the front of my robe for my ordination. The thread that she used to sew them on was still on the robe in bits and pieces, but the roses were gone. I looked at him in absolute dismay and exclaimed, "You cut off my roses!"

As I was dreaming this, I was analyzing his action and my conclusion was, "Of course he did. He thought this robe was a gift, and he's a man; men don't wear roses on their robes."

In the dream, he looked at me as though he never heard or saw my dismay. He just matter-of-factly asked me how I used to prepare sermons, and I remembered that it had been hard for me. It was like a painful process of giving birth, and I suddenly wondered if I really wanted to do that again. Before I could answer him, though, he put the robe on me, backed up to look at me, then stated with an emanating sense of approval that it looked good on me.

I woke up and asked God what it meant and heard in my spirit, "This is a new day." As the days developed, He unpacked the meaning of this dream to me. The bottom line . . . the anointing to minister was still on me and would carry a supernatural favor, but in a different way hence the roses being cut off; and God would show me the way step by step as it unfolded. At the time of editing this book, December 2020, I haven't entered that season yet; I'm still in the healing and restoration season. However, I am fully expecting God's plan for me to unfold according to His will and timing.

Leaving Egypt brings complications.

"Then the Egyptians chased after them with all the horses and chariots of Pharaoh, his horsemen and his army, and they overtook them camping by the sea." – Exodus 14:9

God gives Moses and the Israelites the Word to leave, and then He puts it in Pharaoh's heart to chase after them. *"The Lord hardened the heart of Pharaoh, king of Egypt, and he chased after the sons of Israel as the sons of Israel were going out boldly"* (Exodus 14:8). What is up with that, God? Talk about contradictions. *"As Pharaoh drew near, the sons of Israel looked, and behold, the Egyptians were marching after them, and they became very frightened"* (Exodus 14:10).

Have you ever second-guessed yourself? This would seem like a good time for the Israelites to do exactly that. *"Then they said to Moses, 'Is it because there were no graves in Egypt that you have taken us away to die in the wilderness? . . . Is this not the word that we spoke to you in Egypt, saying, leave us alone that we may serve the Egyptians?'"* (Exodus 14:11-12). All of a sudden, "serving the Egyptians" looked like a walk in the park compared to what they were facing in that moment. Had they made a mistake? The truth is, every decision in life, whether God led or not, has its consequences; and not all consequences are pretty. Some can be quite frightening.

My day came when I realized I couldn't get work anywhere, and I had no money for my upcoming truck payment. I also had a payment coming due on my huge student loan debt, as well as the church's student grant that had to be paid back because I had resigned from the church. I had also moved in with my parents as I had nowhere else to go. "God, did I make a mistake? Did I really hear You correctly? You wouldn't expect me to default on my financial responsibilities, would You? You got me into this mess; surely You're going to provide."

The answer for me was "yes" and "no." The answer for Israel and Moses was an emphatic "yes." I was entering my "Midian" wilderness; they were entering their wilderness that led to the Promised Land. These two wildernesses are not the same. Moses can attest to that as he lived through both; and today I realize that you have to live through both in order to even begin to appreciate the depth of the God we serve.

The "Midian" wilderness is accompanied by great loss and often filled with the silence of God; and while you're in it, you are often entirely dependent on other people to fulfill even your most basic needs. Remember, Jethro provided Moses a place to live and put him in charge of his livestock business. Without Jethro, Moses would have been destitute; and as far as we know, until the day God appeared to Moses in the burning bush, He was silent in Moses' life. That would be forty years of silence!

If it hadn't been for Doris Norris coming alongside me during the implosion of the youth ministry in America, offering me a home and support, I could very well have been destitute too. God had a different plan though. The miracle in the "Midian" wilderness is people—the Jethros and the Doris Norrises and their connections and most of all their God-given compassion for the individual who ends up in the "Midian" wilderness. For some "crazy" reason, they feel attracted to the individual who is in a "Midian" wilderness in a very real and personal way—this can only be God. Doris actually pursued me and wouldn't take no for an answer. She was determined to help me even though I wasn't willing to receive her help for the longest time. Similarly, Jethro was determined to keep Moses. When you look back, can you see the Jethros God put in your life? Maybe there's one in your life right now. That's the miracle of the "Midian" wilderness.

The wilderness that leads out of Egypt into the Promised Land is entirely different. Israel entered it with all their possessions and a great amount of wealth they got from the Egyptians. *"But every woman shall ask of her neighbor and the woman who lives in her house, articles of silver and articles of gold, and clothing; and you will put them on your sons and daughters . . . Thus they plundered the Egyptians . . . now the sons of Israel journeyed . . . about six hundred thousand men on foot, aside from children. A mixed multitude also went up with them, along with flocks and herds, a very large number of livestock"* (Exodus 3:22; 12:35-38).

They left as a wealthy mixed multitude. I love the fact that the writer uses the word *mixed* here. Even in the time of Israel, God's invitation to follow Him was extended to *all* people, not just a certain race. Back to the desert though . . . in this particular desert, God was actively, visibly, tangibly, miraculously involved in every detail of their journey night and day. Every day and every night was filled with miracles of all kinds and with His tangible presence in the form of a cloud by day and a pillar of fire by night. Yes, the Israelites were visibly accompanied by the glory of God. No silence in this desert!

For forty years, Moses had heard nothing from God, but now he got to speak face to face to God, and even saw his form and heard His audible voice, every day. God reveals this in Numbers 12:8 to Miriam and Aaron: *"With him I speak mouth to mouth, even openly, and not in dark sayings, and he beholds the form of the Lord."* Why is it that today, even though we live in a superior covenant to the one in which Moses lived, we don't have this privilege on a daily basis? Yes, people still have theophany experiences today all over the world, but this was the modus operandi between Moses and God *every day! Wow!* I ache to know God like that. Don't you?

The Israelites were whining and crying and complaining, and the Egyptians were gaining on them when God said to Moses, *"Why are you crying out to Me?"* (Exodus 14:15). I was whining and crying and complaining too, because my whole world was falling apart around me. The due date for my truck payment was getting closer; God was not providing, and I wasn't getting any closer to finding a job either, even though I was actively looking. I knew I was going to have to put my pride in my pocket and return my truck to the bank before the due date; so I did. That was a very humbling experience; actually, in the frame of mind I was in, it was a humiliating experience. Pharaoh was coming after me, and I felt broken and defeated. I was also very prideful; that's why it was humiliating. I would go into my prayer closet and just sit there and cry; all I could say to the Lord was, "I have nothing to say." Repercussions can sometimes be quite overwhelming and paralyzing.

But even in "Midian," some miracles erupt through people that give hope and the ability to persevere. In Moses' case, he was given a career as a shepherd and a wife and children, as well as a mentor in Jethro, which helped him forget and move on for forty years. In my case, a woman in Germany whom I've never met heard of my plight and paid my student debt in full; I have no idea who she is. My grandmother, the entrepreneurial spirit that she was, called the Dutch Reformed Church office and negotiated down the amount I owed on my grant and paid it; she also paid for two different flights to America so that I could make a new beginning. I so much wanted to pay her back, but never had the opportunity as she passed away before I could.

"Why are you crying out to Me? Tell the sons of Israel to go forward. As for you, lift up your staff and stretch out your hand over the sea and divide it, and the sons of Israel shall go through the midst of the sea on dry land" (Exodus 14:15). This reminds me of Hebrews 12:1, *"Let us run with endurance the race that is set before us,"* and Hebrews 12:12-13, *"Therefore strengthen the hands that are weak and the knees that are feeble, and make straight paths for your feet, so that the limb which is lame may not be put out of joint, but rather be healed."*

It takes courageous conviction to keep going forward when darkness is throwing everything, including the proverbial kitchen sink, at you.

And don't forget *yourself*... yes, in the midst of it all, *you* get to deal with all your own demons and shortcomings and fears as well. Behind you, Pharaoh is gaining on you, around you are the whirlwinds of fear and anxieties and your own shortcomings, and in front of you is what looks like insurmountable obstacles. Then God says, "What's wrong with you? Move!" Welcome to God's boot camp of faith!

Egypt and Israel finally recognize God as "The Lord."

*God, furthermore, said to Moses, 'Thus you shall say to the sons of Israel, **The Lord**, the God of your fathers, the God of Abraham, the God of Isaac, and the God of Jacob, has sent me to you. This is My name forever, and this is My memorial-name to all generations.'" –* Exodus 3:15

*"At the morning watch, **the Lord** looked down on the army of the Egyptians through the pillar of fire and cloud and brought the army of the Egyptians into confusion. He caused their chariot wheels to swerve, and He made them drive with difficulty; so the Egyptians said, 'Let us flee from Israel, for **the Lord** is fighting for them against the Egyptians.'" –* Exodus 14:24-25

*"Thus **the Lord** saved Israel that day from the hand of the Egyptians, and Israel saw the Egyptians dead on the seashore. When Israel saw the great power which the Lord had used against the Egyptians, **the people feared the Lord**, and **they believed in the Lord** and in His servant Moses." –* Exodus 14:30-31

At last the Egyptians came to grips with the fact that Israel's God was "The Lord." At last, they knew there was no other God like Him. *"Let us flee from Israel, for **the Lord** is fighting for them against the Egyptians."* Why is it that it often takes calamity to get people to recognize their fallibility and to come to the realization that there is only one Divine Authority governing this universe? It took significant death and destruction before Egypt and Israel would even begin to recognize and admit the authority and sovereignty of "The Lord."

What was left of Egypt would have to come to terms with this new revelation, and Israel would have to continue her wilderness journey of faith into the heart of "The Lord." And every nation she bumped into on her journey would also have to reckon with "The Lord." I, too, was and still am on a journey into and from the heart of the Lord, hence the sub title of this book.

Egypt is an extreme example of calamity caused by "The Lord." This is not the norm for God—especially not God as we find Him in the New Testament; but in Egypt's case, it was necessary for "The Lord" to match powers with the "god," Pharaoh, and demonstrate who was truly God. It was necessary for the salvation of Egypt and Pharaoh.

The story leaves Egypt in shambles and follows Israel into the wilderness. One can only hope that Egypt and its Pharaoh took "The Lord" to heart. I believe every nation, in this lifetime, will have its day of reckoning with "The Lord," just like Egypt and Pharaoh. I believe South Africa, and especially the White Afrikaner and the Dutch Reformed Church, had such a visitation; but as a nation in its entirety, they chose their own agenda above God's, causing a shaking that has left great brokenness in its wake. South Africa is reeling in the shambles of denying Christ, living the consequences of sin.

Apartheid, which was a government-sanctioned form of racism, was destructive and divisive. Many voices, both Black and White, cried out against it; but the cries fell on deaf ears. And even though apartheid is abolished, racism still abounds, not just between Black and White, but also between different Black tribes. Racism begets hatred begets violence begets a world where love grows cold. *"Because lawlessness is increased, most people's love will grow cold"* (Matthew 24:12).

It is my prayer that a remnant in South Africa will wake up to a new day in Christ and become His yielded vessels to bring restoration and reconciliation to a country groaning under the weight of lawlessness as a consequence of denying God. Racism is spiritual at its root.

I believe that America is having a visitation right now in 2020 going into 2021, in the midst of a pandemic and racial upheaval. She too as a nation has left her first love, exposing the nation to ruthless forces of darkness. America, as a nation, is experiencing the escalating consequences of a God-forsaken society. My prayer is that she, as a nation, chooses God soon, because time is running out; and the alternative will leave her in shambles.

I can also only pray that the little congregation I left behind in shambles actually took "The Lord" to heart. I pray that my own fallible humanity did not become a stumbling block for them on their road to salvation. And as I journey through my own "Midian" wilderness, I pray that the faithful ones I left behind found restoration and comfort in "The Lord."

"So then, my beloved . . . work out your salvation with fear and trembling; for it is God who is at work in you, both to will and to work for His good pleasure." – Philippians 2:12-13

CHAPTER 10

Emmanuel, God With Us

"Have I not commanded you? Be strong and courageous! Do not tremble or be dismayed, **for the Lord your God is with you wherever you go.**" – Joshua 1:9

"The Lord is the one who goes ahead of you; **He will be with you.** He will not fail you or forsake you. Do not fear or be dismayed." – Deuteronomy 31:8

"Behold, the virgin shall be with child and shall bear a Son, and they shall call his name Immanuel, which translated means, '**God with us.'**" – Matthew 1:23

Israel sets out on a daunting journey into an unknown wilderness with God and His messenger called Moses, to find their Promised Land. "*Then*

Moses led Israel from the Red Sea, and they went out into the wilderness of Shur" (Exodus 15:22). When I read this Scripture, I like to close my eyes and try to imagine being part of a great multitude of people walking through an arid desert with a supernatural cloud leading us and shading us against the sun by day, and a supernatural fire hovering over us at night, keeping us warm and protected from the cold desert nights (Exodus 13:21-22). I try to imagine the surroundings and the smells and the sounds and the sunrises and sunsets and the mindset.

In my imagination, I see a multitude of mixed people of different races. They are men, women, children and livestock, all with one goal in mind: "Follow Moses because he hears the voice of God, and ultimately God is the One leading us, hence the cloud and the pillar of fire. Whatever you do, don't lose sight of Moses and the supernatural phenomena, and don't go astray from this group. Our life depends on staying together and following the man of God." Israel's only point of contact with God was the supernatural phenomena and Moses. Ultimately, God was their only source and hope for entering the Promised Land.

As I imagine this mixed multitude of people dreaming of their "Promised Land," a question arises in my spirit: "What does the 'Promised Land' mean to you, dear one, as you read this book?" During the implementation of apartheid in South Africa, a big movement of White Afrikaner Nationalists believed that South Africa was their "Promised Land" and that they were the "chosen ones." After the abolishment of apartheid, a big movement of Black Nationalists believed that South Africa had become *their* "Promised Land" and that *they* were now the "chosen ones." South Africa went from apartheid to affirmative action in a heartbeat, but ironically segregation and violence continued eating away at the fabric of society, destroying the very "Promised Land" that was supposed to be God's gift to the new "chosen ones."

Mankind has yet to discover the true meaning of the "Promised Land" as applied to a modern society through the lens of Jesus Christ? The "Promised Land", dear one, is no longer a geographical place or socio-economic status or social justice stance, it has evolved through Christ into a state of the heart, a mindset called the kingdom mindset which has the soul of nations (people) at heart? *"Go therefore and make disciples of all the nations"* (Matthew 28:19).

At this point of the journey, Moses was a kind of "Emmanuel" for Israel. He was a forerunner for Christ and acted as the middleman between Israel and God and the surrounding nations. Moses helped facilitate the demonstration of God's redemptive heart to a world bent on destruction. Israel was to be a testimony of God's great and wonderful works. If only Israel and the surrounding nations of that time had laid down their selfish ways and paid attention to the one true source of healing and reconciliation. Instead an entire generation of people died in the wilderness, and many nations were judged by the living God.

Today, as we journey through this world, Christ is Emmanuel, and we follow Christ through His compass called Holy Spirit and His Word, called the Bible. Christ is with us, through his Holy Spirit and the Word, leading the way, all the way into God and from God, establishing His Kingdom on earth as it is in heaven, the "Promised Land"; offering the only legitimate solution for healing and reconciliation between people and God and people groups with each other.

I remember one particular day when this knowledge of Emmanuel started to sink deep into my spirit, and I knew that no matter how lonely the journey, Jesus was right there. It happened at the end of my second year at seminary. I was the designated spiritual leader for a group of students doing evangelism work down at the ocean amongst people on their December vacation. This was a very special time of the year down at this small, private beach nestled into the mountains. It was visited by an eclectic conglomeration of affluent and not-so-affluent White people for the December holidays. Some people landed on the beach in their own private helicopters and lived in their own private beach homes, while others arrived in their vehicles—some expensive and others all beat up—setting up their tents side by side in the campsite. For a couple of weeks, nobody cared about status except, of course, race. The only Blacks present were the maids that came with the affluent White families.

I loved the beach atmosphere. The students that came that year were exceptionally talented. They put on a puppet show on the beach every day with a sound system, and they were so good that even the adults would stop everything they were doing to look and listen. After the puppet show, they would engage the children in all kinds of activities.

My role was to counsel the students, lead the Sunday services in the chapel, and preach on the beach. The services in the chapel were always packed. In the last service I led, the people even sat behind me on the stage. I barely had room to stand. In many ways, it was electrifying. In that atmosphere, nobody cared that I was a woman preaching from the pulpit. However, in the midst of all of that, I felt extremely alone. I had one more year of seminary and no clear vision of my future. A woman in the ministry just wasn't appealing to the Dutch Reformed masses. Everybody that had opposed my studying theology and becoming a minister was looking at me with those "I told you so" looks, and I was wondering what was going to happen to me. Preaching to a full house and being embraced with so much enthusiasm was such a contradiction to my life back at university.

I was in my room one afternoon praying while the students were out enjoying some much-earned play time when I was overcome with a sense of sorrow; tears began to flow. All of a sudden, the face of Jesus appeared on the wall. He looked at me with peace and calmness without once engaging me—He just stayed there for the longest time. It felt if a student had not interrupted us, He might have just stayed right on and right on. If I remember correctly, it was close to an hour that He silently remained as I cried. I have never forgotten it.

The Dutch Reformed Church never taught on supernatural interactions with Christ or heaven. We were taught that the Word was enough, so I had no frame of reference for Jesus' presence entering my room when I was a teenager and inviting me to follow Him as a friend, and I also had no frame of reference for this appearance. For years, I didn't really know what it meant until He finally revealed that it meant, "I am with you wherever you go" (Joshua 1:9).

I learned from the teachings of the Dutch Reformed Church that the Bible is extremely important, and I am so grateful for the formal Biblical training I received. However, I also learned from the Lord Himself that if the Bible does not launch you into a personal relationship with Jesus and His Holy Spirit, then all you have are letters on pages which result in a legalistic academic doctrine without the power and intimacy of the Author. The Book must lead you to the Author, or else you will end up in legalism; or you'll dismiss the contents as just another religious world view. I am humbled that the Author has revealed Himself to me the way He has, but I am also ruined by those encounters, because I ache for more of Him on a daily basis.

God wooed Israel with His presence and power in the wilderness, while Israel grumbled and complained all the way.

"And behold, the glory of the Lord appeared in the cloud . . . I have heard the grumblings of the sons of Israel; speak to them, saying, 'At twilight you shall eat meat and in the morning you shall be filled with bread; and you shall know that I am the Lord your God.'" – Exodus 16:10, 12

Over and over and over Israel met with challenges as they travelled through the wilderness and, instead of trusting the Lord to provide, they would start moaning and groaning and murmuring and threatening Moses and Aaron and reminiscing about the "good ole days" back in Egypt. They never did comprehend that they were safe in the arms of God and that this same God was testing their allegiance and faith in Him with these challenges (Exodus 15:25). The tests were there to determine whether Israel could be trusted to remain faithful and devoted to God in the midst of a generous gift like the Promised Land. If they could learn to trust God and have faith and joy during challenging times in the wilderness, then certainly they would stay faithful to Him when immersed in the abundance of the Promised Land, because only then would they remember Who the source of their abundance was: *"Beware that you do not forget the Lord your God, for it is He who is giving you power to make wealth . . . otherwise when you have eaten and are satisfied, and have built good houses and lived in them . . . then your heart will become proud and you will forget the Lord your God who brought you out from the land of Egypt, out of the house of slavery"* (Deuteronomy 8:11-12, 14).

You see, abundance and affluence tend to corrupt the human soul, but the memory of God providing in the wilderness guards and protects the soul against corruption during the times of abundance, because it constantly reminds the human soul Who the source of the abundance is. The truth is, if you can't be faithful and steadfast in the wilderness, you will never be able to faithfully and steadfastly steward God's Promised Land, which comes loaded with His blessing. *"You shall remember all the way which the Lord your God has led you in the wilderness these forty years, that He might humble you, testing you, to know what was in your heart, whether you would keep His commandments or not. He humbled you and let you be hungry, and fed you with manna which you did not know, nor did your fathers know, that he might make you understand that man does not live by bread alone, but man lives by everything that proceeds out of the mouth of the Lord"* (Deuteronomy 8:2-3).

If you look at Israel's history in the Bible, the generation of Joshua is probably the only generation that came anywhere near making a success of affluence and blessings. The rest of the generations, once they entered seasons of affluence and blessing, always ended in self-seeking righteousness and corruption and sin, with Solomon and his generation being the epitome of failing to steward God's blessings. Israel also never got it right to successfully transfer the heritage of blessing that was on one generation to the next. The next generation, who was raised in the affluent blessings of the previous generation, would always forget God and end up reeling in the shambles of sin, eventually perishing in their rejection of God. *"But you shall remember the Lord your God, for it is He who is giving you power to make wealth, that He may confirm His covenant which He swore to your fathers, as it is this day. It shall come about if you ever forget the Lord your God and go after other gods and serve them and worship them, I testify against you today that you will surely perish."* (Deuteronomy 8:18-19).

It is important in this day and age that we as a church not only enter and steward God's Promised Land, which is the kingdom of God deposited into the hearts of people, but also remain faithful right to the very end. We need to end well too. We need to empower the next generation to go even deeper into God than we did. History is full of revivals where a generation was rocked by the presence and power of God, but every revival eventually petered out and just became great stories in dusty church history books, totally forgotten by the next generation. The blessed generation failed to pass the baton effectively, and the next generation failed to capitalize on the momentum of the revival in the previous generation. And most of all, the revivals failed to sustainably disciple and transform the hearts of society!

However, I am convinced that a generation is rising up that will embrace God fully and represent His kingdom and His righteousness on this earth in every aspect of society, as it is in heaven, right to their very last breath. ***They will live and end well and pass the baton with sustainable momentum.*** Acts 2 is just a foretaste of what is to come. The full prophesy of Joel is yet to unfold (Acts 2:16-18). We have yet to see God's spirit fall on ALL people (Christian and non-Christian alike), and we have yet to see ALL God's sons and daughters prophesying.

In spite of Israel's whining and complaining at every challenge in the wilderness, God still miraculously provided every time, wooing them into embracing Him as their Lord. He was after their heart and their allegiance. Read the rest of Exodus and Deuteronomy. It is quite remarkable just how many supernatural demonstrations this generation of Israel and the surrounding nations saw and experienced on a very personal level. I am quite jealous! This generation of mixed people called

Israel was supposed to become one new nation in God, a testimony to the other nations of His great and wonderful works. Before they could steward a gift like the Promised Land, they needed to know the God of the Land, and God was pulling out all the stops to demonstrate who He was so that they would embrace Him. Sadly, they failed to trust Him and acknowledge Him, and the entire generation, except for Joshua and Caleb, perished in the wilderness, leaving it up to the next generation to enter and steward the ultimate gift of the Promised Land in partnership with the God of the Covenant.

Oh, my goodness, how many times over the years have I failed this test of trust myself? How about you? It is not easy to trust for provision when there is none, without becoming anxious and whiney and "complainey" and throwing tantrums. The process of keeping the joy of the Lord, trusting Him when you are scared to death, or offering God sacrifices of praise as a gift of trust and acknowledgement when you'd rather give Him a grocery list of complaints can be quite brutal; but I've learned that trusting and acknowledging Him is a step that cannot be skipped on our way into and from His heart. Our own hearts and the hearts of others cannot be transformed without it.

I've learned from Him that if I want to enter His Promised Land called the Kingdom and truly see healing and reconciliation and favor on a personal and national and international level, I have to doggedly, joyfully, worshipfully and thankfully practice trust in Him no matter what life throws at me. *He will provide! He is with me wherever I go!* Say this out loud: "He is with me wherever I go." Repeat it as often as needed.

"Be anxious for nothing, but in everything by prayer and supplication with thanksgiving let your requests be made known to God. And the peace of God, which surpasses all comprehension, will guard your hearts and your minds in Christ Jesus." (Philippians 4:6). Israel had the wrong end of the stick, which was, "Be anxious for everything!" Don't let this ring true in your own life. Rather, let this truth sink in: "God is with you wherever you go!"

Behold, the mountain of God!

"Behold, I stand at the door and knock; if anyone hears My voice and opens the door, I will come in to him and will dine with him, and he with Me." – Revelation 3:20

"Then Moses went up with Aaron, Nadab and Abihu, and seventy of the elders of Israel, and they saw the God of Israel; and under His feet there appeared to be a pavement of sapphire, as clear as the sky itself. Yet He did not stretch out His hand against the nobles of the sons of Israel; and they saw God and they ate and drank." – Exodus 24:9-11

The mountain of God is a very special place of intimacy with God. It is the place where we stop to meet with Him and be equipped and anointed by Him. It is that personal space where man and God tarry together, and His Spirit of wisdom and revelation transforms and encourages our hearts. It is the prayer closet of seasoned prayer warriors; it is the serendipitous moments of special intimate encounters with the living God; it is the public assemblies where God displays His presence and power to groups of people; it is anywhere and everywhere that His presence is acknowledged, and man and God commune.

Jethro visits Moses at the mountain.

"Then Jethro, Moses' father-in-law, came with his sons and his wife to Moses in the wilderness where he was camped, at the mount of God." – Exodus 18:5

The writer of Exodus just matter-of-factly mentions Jethro here and there. However, I don't think we can even begin to appreciate the role that this man played in Moses' life. God caused Jethro to strategically enter Moses life twice. The first time Jethro entered his life, Moses was fleeing from Pharaoh. With this first meeting, Jethro came to Moses' aid and offered him a place of refuge in the form of his home and family. With the second meeting, Jethro came to the mountain and spoke into Moses' life in a way that transformed Moses' leadership style which affected the entire nation in a very good way. Read Exodus 18. There at the mountain, Jethro taught Moses how to delegate authority and therefore govern a huge multitude much more effectively.

Even at the mountain, God uses special people in profound ways in our lives, and it would behoove us to be sensitive in recognizing those people and actually embracing and applying their advice for however long they accompany us on our journey. As I've mentioned before, Doris Norris was one such person who came alongside me for a season in America and profoundly touched me and aided in my spiritual journey into and from the heart of God.

I, too, found myself in a strange country, just like Moses did when he fled from Pharaoh, licking the wounds that had been inflicted upon me during my ministry in South Africa and the youth ministry in America. I felt spiritually devastated. Today, looking back, I realize I was in shock when Doris first met me. I had been as faithful as I knew how to be to the Lord I loved so much; and yet, everything I did for Him and hopefully through Him in South Africa and America had come and was coming to naught. In my mind, I was a total failure.

The first time I saw Doris, she was weaving through a small group at a church Bible study that I was attending for the first time, zooming in on me. I found out later that this was the Doris way. She apprehended new people and loved them into staying and feeling welcome. This great-grandmother's hugs were anointed and infectious. She embraced and loved people with her pastor's heart, and they responded.

Not I! Well, maybe I did respond a little bit, but she had to work harder than usual for my attention. However, that didn't seem to intimidate her at all. She seemed oblivious to my "coldness" and determined to corral me in. Before I knew what hit me, I went home with her and her husband, Elwood, for lunch that day, and a month or two later, I was living with them in their home. I still don't really know what hit me.

Doris changed my perception of the Lord forever. She introduced me to theologians like Bill Johnson, Randy Clark, Patricia King, Bishop Garlington, and so many more. She took me to conferences where these theologians taught and ministered. She exposed me to the kind of intimacy with the Lord that I thought had died with the people we read about in the pages of the Bible. Doris rocked my spiritual world, and I received and drank and slowly, very slowly, healed.

Elwood was special too. Even though he didn't quite understand Doris's spiritual hunger and deep intimacy with the Lord, he recognized the validity of it and nurtured it. Elwood loved "Mama," and he allowed her the space to serve the Lord in very special ways. He actually sacrificed his own comfort often for the sake of her spiritual activities. She was always seeking more of the Lord.

Elwood loved the Lord, but according to him, "Mama knew the Lord." If you needed a breakthrough in anything in your life, according to Elwood Norris, just ask Doris to pray—it'll happen. One day he and I were talking about the Second World War and his duties in France when he said something very memorable. Some of Elwood's friends never made it home, but he did; and he told me the only reason he made it home was because "Mama prayed." Another very popular saying of his was, "If Mama not happy, nobody happy." Oh, they were a hoot! They demonstrated unconditional love to me. They were part of God's salvation and restoration in my life. I think I can safely say that Moses felt that way about Jethro too even at the mountain where God's presence could have seemed suffice.

God formally affirms his man before Israel.

"The Lord said to Moses, 'Behold, I will come to you in a thick cloud, so that the people may hear when I speak with you and may also believe in you forever' . . . And Moses brought the people out of the camp to meet God, and they stood at the foot of the mountain. Now Mount Sinai was all in smoke . . . When the sound of the trumpet

grew louder and louder, Moses spoke and God answered him with thunder." – Exodus 19: 9, 17-19

The great "I AM," the Lord, came down to affirm the messenger, Moses, in front of the whole of Israel with fire and smoke in a thick cloud. This reminds me of the moment when Jesus came out of the water after being baptized by John the Baptist. There God opened the windows of heaven and affirmed Jesus in front of everybody, by causing the Spirit of God to descend and light on Him in the form of a dove while saying from heaven, *"This is My beloved Son, in whom I am well pleased."*

Wow! The great I AM formally affirmed His messengers before great crowds of witnesses. Moses and Jesus hosted Holy Spirit in such an authoritative way while displaying absolute humbleness and obedience, absolute oneness with the great I AM and He with them. It should be every child of God's desire to host God in this fashion. *"Truly, truly, I say to you, he who believes in Me, the works that I do, he will do also; and greater works than these he will do; because I go to the Father"* (John 14:12).

God wants us to be known as His disciples!

God's glory cloud

"The Lord said to Moses, 'Behold, I will come to you in a thick cloud.'" – Exodus 19:9

"Then the house, the house of the Lord, was filled with a cloud, so that the priests could not stand to minister because of the cloud, for the glory of the Lord filled the house of God." - 2 Chronicles 5:13 and 14

The first time I encountered the glory cloud, I once again had no frame of reference for it. I was praying late one night in my bedroom. Elwood had passed away, and I was taking care of Doris. By that time, she was fighting the last stages of congestive heart failure and kidney failure. While I was praying, a cloud started to form against the far side of my bedroom where the wall and the ceiling met, and inside the cloud were multitudes and multitudes of sparkles. The cloud and the sparkles were mesmerizing, and even though I had no frame of reference for it, I knew exactly what it was. I was in awe and just worshiped God while I feasted my eyes on the cloud and the sparkles. This was the first of several similar occasions in my bedroom.

And while we are on the topic of God's glory, I had a different kind of encounter with His glory one afternoon that also left me mesmerized. I was sitting on the front porch enjoying the beauty of spring, when the atmosphere changed all of a sudden. The yard consisted of big trees and green lawn and the neighborhood itself was in full bloom; it was a beautiful time of the year. The colors were awesome, and as I looked at the trees and the rest of the surroundings, the Lord demonstrated an aspect of His glory to me that left me once again in awe. All of a sudden, the trees and the leaves literally started breathing, and it looked like they were softly swaying back and forth. The colors popped into an indescribable beauty and vibrancy, and light shone through the gaps and around everything. Everything was illuminated, vibrant, alive and spectacular.

The neat thing about it was, I could look at my surroundings in the natural, and then I could look at it in the glory. I was able to go back and forth between the natural and the glory. A joy welled up in me, and I just drank it in with a great big Cheshire cat smile on my face. That experience on the porch has never happened again, and it's not something I can conjure up either. It was totally God's pleasure to reveal His glory to me. All I can say is, *"Lord, our Lord, how majestic is your name in all the earth!"* (Psalm 8:9).

"All the people perceived the thunder and the lightning flashes and the sound of the trumpet and the mountain smoking; and when the people saw it they trembled and stood at a distance. Then they said to Moses, 'Speak to us yourself and we will listen; but let not God speak to us, or we will die.' Moses said to the people, 'Do not be afraid; for God has come in order to test you, and I order that the fear of Him may remain with you, so that you may not

sin.' So the people stood at a distance, while Moses approached the thick cloud where God was" (Exodus 20:18-21).

It is too bad the people did not want to personally hear God's voice. That was the difference between them and Moses and people like Joshua and Caleb. The people knew God through Moses, but Moses and people like Joshua and Caleb knew God personally and intimately. If only they'd had a hunger to know the Lord intimately themselves. I believe if they had, the journey would have been quite different. Instead they hung their fears and displeasures and accusations on the shoulders of Moses, eventually pulling him down with them into a wilderness grave. If your relationship with the Lord stops at the Word and the person ministering the Word to you on Sundays or at Bible Studies, you will falter and eventually peter out. The power and the blessing and the revelation of His Promised Land called the Kingdom of God, is in His presence.

Moses dies, and Joshua and the next generation of Israel have to move on without him.

"So Moses the servant of the lord died there in the land of Moab, according to the word of the Lord . . . So the sons of Israel wept for Moses in the plains of Moab thirty days; then the days of weeping and mourning for Moses came to an end." – Deuteronomy 34:5, 8

"Now it came about after the death of Moses the servant of the Lord, that the Lord spoke to Joshua the son of Nun, Moses servant saying, 'Moses, my servant is dead; now therefore arise, cross this Jordan, you and all this people, to the land which I am giving to them, to the sons of Israel.'" – Joshua 1:1-2

Saying farewell to a leader like Moses could not have been easy, and Joshua must have been terrified stepping into his shoes. Moses had laid hands on Joshua, causing God's spirit of wisdom to come upon him. Israel recognized the anointing on him and embraced him as their next leader

(Deuteronomy 34:9). For thirty days, they mourned the loss of Moses, and then God spoke to Joshua and told him it was time to move forward. The time had come for Joshua and the next generation to cross the Jordan and take the Promised Land: *"Every place on which the sole of your foot treads, I have given it to you, just as I spoke to Moses"* (Joshua 1:3).

Great promise and victory lay ahead. However, I think it's wonderful that God gave them thirty days to first mourn their loss before requiring they move on. God knew their hearts were broken, and He had the compassion to give them time to process their loss and come to terms with it.

Five months before writing this chapter, I had to say goodbye to Doris. She had taken a turn for the worse in November 2015 and slowly spiraled down till she passed away the end of March 2016. She was ninety-two years old. Her passing was a shock to me, even though I knew it was inevitable. I wanted God to heal Doris. I understand and know that we all have to die at some point, but I refuse to accept that we have to die from sickness and disease. *"Although Moses was one hundred and twenty years old when he died, his eye was not dim, nor his vigor abated"* (Deuteronomy 34:7). Moses lived in a lesser covenant than we do. Did Jesus not say that we would do the things that He did and greater things? We live in a superior covenant!

When Doris took a turn for the worse, I began a five-week fast. I fasted every other day and ate just one small meal the days in between. I knew I couldn't go on a full fast because I had to keep up my strength to take care of Doris; but I was determined to bang down heaven's doors on her behalf. Can I tell you a little secret? There's no need to bang on heaven's doors. They are already open in Christ. Sometimes we just don't like the answer to our prayers.

Every day when I took time to pray for her during the five weeks, the Lord would give me the same vision. It was an empty field that was charred to the ground. As far as my eye could see, it was black and burned out. I knew the Lord's answer to my prayer for Doris's healing was "no" based on the vision, but I was determined to wrestle with Him. I wanted that field to turn green. I was exhausted, but I wasn't about to give up. Every free moment that I had, I wrestled with Him in prayer; but the field never changed. When Doris died, I collapsed.

Taking care of Doris and Elwood over the years had taken a toll on my health, and my wrestling with the Lord for the last several months of Doris's life put the final pieces together for a major collapse. I spent the next five months fighting a raging systemic attack that left me completely exhausted.

On Thursday, August 18, 2016, I reached rock bottom. I was so sick that I did not think I would live another day. And on that day, I had an encounter with the Lord. I was at a prayer meeting, just barely holding it together. Louisiana was flooded, and people were devastated; I had been praying for them all week. While I was praying at this prayer meeting, I found myself flying in a vision over the flooded region with the Lord, assessing the damage and the devastation. All of a sudden, I became terribly overwhelmed by it all. When the Lord saw how overwhelmed I was, He took me up and up and up, far away from the floods and devastation, to a place that was filled with peace and tranquility and beauty. His presence and the beauty that surrounded me filled me with so much peace and serenity.

While I was bathing in the Lord's presence and the serenity of the place, the bottom opened. As I looked down, I could once again see the flood and devastation. While I was looking at it, I heard the Lord say, "Marlene, you can stay here, or you can go back. The choice is yours." A part of me was very tempted to stay, but I looked at the devastation below and answered, "If you will anoint me with the ability to come up with solutions that will bring comfort and restoration to situations like that (looking at the flood) and actually anoint me to make a difference in people's lives, bring healing to a world in pain, then I want to go back. But if I'm going to stay helpless and hopeless and sick like I feel at the moment, then I want to stay." He didn't say anything, the vision ended and the prayer meeting continued.

I went home that night and went through one of the worst nights so far. It was so bad I really thought I was going to die. Since I had no insurance or the ability to pay for medical help and was really too sick to help myself, I came to terms with the fact that death was okay if it happened. At five the following morning, the acute illness abruptly stopped, giving me a reprieve for about a month. Later, the sickness came back, and I've been dealing with it ever since, but I have hope too. Will Jesus anoint me to become a solution to brokenness? Will He answer my prayer? I am still here! The fact that you are reading this book, dear one, means you are still here. Christ's work of redemption and healing through you and me is not done.

"Then Joshua rose early in the morning; and he and all the sons of Israel set out . . ." (Joshua 3:1). By God's grace, I am rising and I, too, stand at my Jordan, waiting to cross over to the Promised Land of partnering with Holy Spirit and representing His kingdom and His righteousness on this earth as it is in heaven in a tangible form of redemption and healing. And once again, God has positioned people around me to help me make the transition.

I don't know what lies on the other side of my Jordan, but I do know this: God is with me wherever I go!

"Be strong and courageous! Do not tremble or be dismayed, for the Lord your God is with you wherever you go." – Joshua 1:9

"If you abide in Me, and My words abide in you, ask whatever you wish, and it will be done for you." – John 15:7

I am not there yet, but I sure ain't where I used to be either! I am on my way! How about you?

"Brethren, I do not regard myself as having laid hold of it yet; but one thing I do: forgetting what lies behind and reaching forward to what lies ahead, I press on toward the goal for the prize of the upward call of God in Christ Jesus." – Philippians 3:13-14

CHAPTER 11

The Great I Am and His Uniting Power of Agape Love

*"Then Joshua rose early in the morning; and he and **all the sons of Israel set out [united/as one]** . . ."* (Joshua 3:1).

*"The glory which you have given Me [Jesus] I have given to them, **that they may be one, just as We are one**; I in them and You in Me, that they may be perfected in unity, so that the world may know that You sent Me, and loved them, even as You have loved Me."* – John 17:22,23.

The generation of Israelites that left Egypt never understood the power of unity and what it truly meant to be one people serving under the Great I AM. They perished in ignorance. However, in the midst of that generation, another one was rising, one that crossed the Jordan and occupied the Promised Land with Joshua. They were 100 percent united under the great I AM in sync with Joshua and the elders of Israel. This is the only generation of Israelites in the Bible that truly understood what it meant to be one people under God. Together they conquered, occupied and transformed the hearts of people in the Promised Land, demonstrating the heart of God. There is a victorious transformational power that can only be unlocked through a people united in God . . .

While preparing for a sermon on unity, I found myself reading John 17. There we find Jesus praying in front of His disciples for Himself, His disciples, the future church and the world. The main focus of His prayer is unity, and when you read His prayer, it becomes obvious that unity is powerful. Everything rises and falls in the presence or the absence of unity. But not all unity is equal. Holy Spirit started challenging me to think about that: not all unity is equal. As a matter of fact, some unions are downright evil. So, the question started arising in me, what makes a union legit in God's eyes? What makes people unite and why do some unions have God's blessing and others don't?

Three words jumped out at me when I read John 17: 22 and 23: *glory, perfected,* and *loved.* We all like to think that love unites, but did you know that love can also divide? All forms of love have powerful repercussions, whether positive or negative, but did you know that only one meets all of God's requirements? Only one can actually give true meaning to the words "glory" and "perfected."

Eros love

Eros is one of the words in the Bible used for love. It's the most basic kind of love. In its simplest form, it is demonstrated by two people coming together for the pleasure of making love. It's filled with romance, passion, intimacy. It's the kind that says, "I only have eyes for you."

Doris and Elwood were in their eighties and Elwood would never leave the room without touching Doris. Whenever he went to the store, he always came back with flowers for mama. In turn, when he came home from work, he would sit down in his easy chair, and Doris would go upstairs and get his slippers. She would come downstairs, remove his shoes and put on his slippers and kiss him on his forehead and tell him what a wonderful husband he was.

We had a women's conference at church once, and some of the younger women wanted Doris to speak on sex because they wanted to know if sex flew out the door when you got older. Doris gave an unforgettable speech that day, leaving everybody speechless. Let me tell you, Doris and Elwood understood the importance of romance, passion and intimacy in marriage. The Bible book called Song of Solomon is graphically expressive about eros and the fruit of it. Eros, in its pure form, is a gift from God. When eros is practiced in union with God and His intention for it, it's a beautiful thing.

Unfortunately, the devil counterfeits everything that God made in an attempt to blind people and separate them from God. Outside of the context for which God created eros, it quickly starts evolving around personal pleasure and experiences that stroke the ego and make the flesh feel good. Outside of God, eros starts feeding personal sensual needs and very quickly promotes the "self" to replace God. All of a sudden, the union that it was designed to create becomes corrupt, and we end up with pornography, prostitution, rape, promiscuity, child trafficking, abortion and the list goes on.

It also starts seeping into societies in much more subtle and complex invisible ways. All of a sudden, we see individuals uniting around opinions or philosophies or ideologies that tickle their flesh. I'm sure you've heard the saying, "Birds of a feather flock together." When this happens, we find people gravitating towards homogenous groups because they all agree, and that agreement makes them feel good and safe; it tickles their fleshly, sensual desires, and if you don't agree with them, you're not welcome. All activities are planned and centered around a self-serving opinion or philosophy. If you don't comply, there's the door, Jack, and don't look back. The gist is, conform or leave. Conformity, though, is not unity. Conformity denies diversity, whereas unity celebrates diversity. As a matter of fact, true unity cannot exist without diversity.

Let's do a little experiment to bring this point home. Let's put one self-serving republican amongst a group of self-serving democrats or one self-serving democrat amongst a group of self-serving republicans and make them do life together. What do you think the outcome is going to be? Will you still find that lonesome republican or democrat with the rest of the group a year later? I think it's safe to say no, unless they've somehow been shackled into slavery.

Why? Because conformed units are based on a self-serving eros philosophy or opinion that causes its members to aggressively protect and fight for self-preservation. These units are often riddled with self-centered competition and lack of trust. They are performance driven, because their members are required to prove their allegiance. The consequences of not conforming can be quite brutal, even to their very own. The political arena is a magnificent illustration of brutal, performance-driven, self-centered, competitive conformity and lack of trust.

Over time, if left unchecked, these arenas evolve into a narcissistic, dog-eat-dog world riddled with betrayal and conflict and rivalry. Sound familiar? Shockingly and sadly, some churches and even some families function this way by pushing rigid, legalistic rules and regulations and performance instead of truth and unconditional love and forgiveness. Oh, my gosh, forgiveness? What's that?

Did I mention a narcissistic, dog-eat-dog world? Narcissism has no comprehension of forgiveness. Narcissism is eros on steroids without God. It has been documented by behavioral scientists and theologians and psychiatrists that narcissists are incapable of tolerating people who are different than them. Anybody who is different becomes the enemy, one of the so-called "them." They look at the world as "I" versus "them," or "we" (our unit) versus "them." The world is full of narcissism. It's what gives rise to things like racism, tribalism, nationalism, cults, clubs, politics, dynasties, unions, even some churches. (Lord, help us.)

And as if that's not enough, pretty soon, "they" or "them," the so-called enemy, becomes an impersonal concept, stripped of all humanity. Instead of disagreeing with Joe as a person, our disagreement makes Joe synonymous with his "wrong" belief, which means Joe is made synonymous with an impersonal concept, which means he isn't human anymore and therefore does not need compassion. I encourage you to chew on that a little bit.

The narcissist eventually becomes incapable of recognizing the personhood of another human being, sometimes even within their own network. So other people become mere mechanical tools or commodities that have somehow been put there to be used and abused and owned, even ridiculed and, if necessary, destroyed for the sake of "me" and "my agenda." Remember Pharaoh enslaving the Hebrews. Remember the judge at the river. Communism, dictatorship, apartheid, slavery, abuse, disrespect, entitlement are just some of the fruits of this kind of narcissism. Even social justice causes, outside of God, fall prey to this.

When I was the Office Manager of the Peace Secretariat in the Free State, I was in a board meeting once in South Africa. The Peace Secretariat was established by the government to help transition South Africa from the old apartheid regime to the new democratic one. In the board meeting, we were discussing the future of South Africa. At one point, a member of the Communist party stood up and addressed the room. He stated very calmly, exuding confidence and extreme intelligence, that the Communists were quite prepared to work alongside the African National Congress (ANC) and bide their time. He stated that it was only a matter of time before the ANC would destroy South Africa, leaving the road wide open for the Communists to step in with their Marxist ideology and socialistic strategies. Later, it became clear that not only would the Communists bide their time, but they would actually encourage division by purposely encouraging racism and violence. As a matter of fact they had their fingers in every bit of South Africa's pie and still do.

The Communists, who have a superior narcissistic agenda of their own, have been capitalizing on the gullibility of narcissistic Black social justice groups and White Nationalists and Supremacists. They dish up social justice on a platter of well-disguised Marxism called socialism, drawing youth and other gullible members of society into their web, polarizing communities. Today, they are still stirring the racism pot while South Africa spirals further and further down into a web of no return, unless God intervenes. If God does not intervene, I predict that South Africa will be swallowed up by Marxism. Another group that's right on the heels of the Marxists in South Africa are the Moslems. Either one, if given the opportunity, will destroy Christianity in a heartbeat. History has also proven that both of these forms of government always end with a dictatorship, causing horrible suffering and hardship for the people who gullibly followed them into their web.

The nuclear family structure is not spared from narcissistic relational games either. How many people live in an abusive family environment because of a narcissistic family member? I know so many sad situations of spouses abusing each other, parents abusing children, children abusing parents, children abusing children . . . the list goes on.

Another word for *abuse* is *bullying*. Society is full of it. How many teachers and pupils are victims of bullies? How many neighborhoods are being terrorized by gangs? How many church people are walking around wounded and bleeding because of abusive, legalistic narcissism in the church? Legalism is a form of entitlement which often lends itself to bullying its own and rejecting those outside. How many unbelievers want nothing to do with church because they've been tried, judged and spat out by so-called believers who found them distasteful and unworthy of their "holy clique," their private, elite religious club?

Eros units are closed cliques united around some common, self-serving denominator and are often extremely powerful and influential and dangerous. I received firsthand experience of this fact whilst ministering amongst White Afrikaner Nationalists and Supremacists and also amongst Black social justice groups in South Africa. Eros units are often quite capable of manipulating entire families, cities, societies or even entire countries to adhere to their agendas. In their quest, everybody else becomes one big, impersonal blur; and "I" or "we, the clique" becomes everything. These individuals recognize the power of unity, and they twist it into a corrupt form of conformity in order to achieve their own self-centered goals and pleasures, even if it means bullying some people into submission and marginalizing or getting rid of others. The enemy is so cunning and the masses are so gullible!

Our pastor conducted a survey in our congregation and was astonished by how many people in our congregation said they were painfully lonely. And it wasn't because of a lack of community or activities or small groups. This was before the COVID-19 lockdowns. The structure was there, the opportunities to relate and connect were available in abundance, so why the loneliness and pain?

Could it be that in spite of churches putting structures and opportunities for community in place that people are still, at least to some degree, functioning on an eros level, concentrating on self? *My* needs, *my* expectations, *my* brokenness, *my* shyness, *my* toes . . . you stepped on *my* toes, *my* feelings, *my* thin skin, *my* sensitivities, *my* life. I want this, *I* want that, *I* can't, *I* won't, *I* am offended . . .

Loneliness and the painful isolation that goes with it is sometimes a consequence of self centered offence. I realize that's not always the case; some people are going through a lonely, painful season because God has put them there or because of some traumatic event in their life that they are processing. Let me encourage you that if you are there right now, it's only for a season. Keep your heart soft and trust God to guide you. By His grace, you will get through it and be better for it. However, sometimes loneliness is caused by unrealistic self centered expectations, which leads to offense and hurt feelings, which causes people to walk away from community. Self centeredness eventually leads to loneliness.

I'm not married, but while counseling married couples, I recognized a certain phenomenon that often presented itself between couples. People often fall in love with somebody based on a fantasy they have of that person, which leads to unrealistic expectations. Their relationship with their spouse is actually between themselves and their own fantasy. It's how I define the honeymoon period. Then, they wake up one day to a stranger, because that person no longer conforms to their fantasy. The honeymoon period is over, and honey ain't so honey anymore. It's at that point when eros has to make room for true love, which the Bible calls agape love. Agape love begins where eros ends. Agape love is the kind of love that stays through thick and thin, for better, for worse, for richer, for poorer, in sickness and in health, through friction, in spite of friction, with friction. Agape love lays self centeredness down.

I heard it said once that community, which is the outward manifestation of unity, isn't community until somebody you don't like shows up. Unity celebrates diversity. Jesus prayed in John 17, asking that our unity become perfected. Unity is perfected through disagreement and friction, and only agape love can navigate the process of perfection. Unfortunately, it's at this point where many couples and communities and even churches fall off the bandwagon, because the majority of people are not prepared to move from self-centered eros love to sacrificial, unconditional agape love.

People who live only by eros love manipulate other people and circumstances in order to serve their own agenda, which leads to distrust, which leads to rejection, which leads to isolation and loneliness and bitterness. It's a vicious cycle that manifests in all kinds of ugly, destructive ways like anger, unforgiveness, addictions, depression and violence. People who major on self-centered eros love are often broken, hurting people; and they very often break and hurt other people. Eros love, even in its purest form, will attract people only for the short term; but in the long run, it won't keep them. Agape love keeps them. True unity is found in the midst of agape love.

So, let's look at Agape love.

"Have this attitude in yourselves which was also in Christ Jesus, who, although He existed in the form of God, did not regard equality with God a thing to be grasped, but emptied Himself, taking the form of a bond-servant and being made in the likeness of men. Being found in appearance as a man, He humbled Himself by becoming obedient to the point of death, even death on a cross." – Philippians 2:5-8

Agape love is sacrificial, unconditional love that voluntarily does life with people who are different and don't necessarily have the same values. Agape love serves all without compromising Godly ways. Jesus is the ultimate example of this. A person full of agape love practices the kind of love that loves God with all their heart and soul and mind and their neighbor as themselves. It's the kind of love that blows their neighbors away because it's not normal. I mean, just think about what unconditional love really means. By nature, we often cruelly criticize ourselves and others, which means our natural, carnal way of loving is conditional.

We need an extra ingredient before unconditional love manifests. That's why Jesus says in John 17:22, *"The glory which You have given Me I have given to them, that they may be one."* Agape love requires the glory of God. Glory is supernatural, which means agape love is supernatural; and the unity that is created through agape love is supernatural. Agape love is patented by God, filled with His Spirit and branded with the name of Jesus. That's why Jesus prays in John 11:17, *"Keep them in your name, the name which You have given Me, that they may be one even as We are."*

Notice that phrase, *"Keep them in your name."* God's glory and His name always go together. The brand of love we choose, is important. When Moses asked God to show him His glory, God went before him proclaiming His name and showing him His goodness. Why His name? The very nature of God is in His name, in the brand. The very nature of God has to reside in us or else we cannot love with agape love. That's why Jesus prays in verse 26, *"I have made Your name [brand] known to them, and will make it known, so that the love with which You loved Me may be in them, and I in them."*

Until you and I become one with the living God, until we actually assimilate His very nature into our beings and become expressions of His name brand, we will not see the fruits of agape love, nor will we see His resurrection power transform and restore people to God's original intent. Just praying in the name of Jesus is not enough; we have to actually be an expression and demonstration of His name in our communities. That requires intimacy with the living God. Can I put it more brashly? You have to actually use and assimilate the brand and not just talk about it. The more intimate we are with God, the more we become like God and the more we become like God, the more society is drawn to Him and His love in us.

The closest a society without God can come to agape love is fileo love, the kind you find between best friends or soulmates. David and Jonathan are biblical examples of fileo love. It's beautiful, special and sacrificial; but it still loves only the people who it considers its own. It's not agape love, but it's a big step up from eros love. Some secular humanistic movements and causes serve pockets of society with fileo love, and they ought to be commended for their contribution to communities. They do a great job, but their foot print in society is still limited by their own human affiliations and prejudices.

King Solomon knew he needed more if he was really going to make a difference leading a stiff-necked nation and so he asked for wisdom to know what that more was. Really, he was asking God to give him access to His heart and His mind. Can I respectfully say, he wanted to be able to pick God's brain at whim as he was challenged by the complexities of making right choices and causing others to do the same? He wanted a spirit of wisdom and revelation in the knowledge of God that Paul talks about in Ephesians 1:17. As long as he submitted to God and God's ways, that's exactly what he got. So much so that the Queen of Sheba, one of the most prominent leaders of that world, observed his leadership style and methods and embraced His God as the author of all of it. She observed Solomon and saw his God.

Solomon knew agape Love Himself and was given a Godly wisdom to create total peace and prosperity within the borders of Israel which transformed one of the most powerful women in the world into a believer. Just imagine how the church today in unison with agape Love Himself, can transform the hearts of cities and communities and leaders. God is extending an invitation to whoever will respond right now. The fact that you are reading this means, the invitation is being extended to you!

Agape Love Himself extended an invitation to Abraham by making a covenant with him in Genesis 17:2 to multiply him and his descendants exceedingly, knowing full well that mankind was corrupt and would consistently choose the curse above the blessing. Still, Agape Love made a covenant with Abraham as opposed to a contract. A contract is a conditional agreement committing to execute a particular promise if the other party keeps their side of the agreement; but if the contract is violated, there is no longer any obligation to execute that promise. In contrast, a covenant is an unconditional agreement, promising to behave a certain way regardless of how the other party behaves.

Agape love does not compromise values but does take chances on people. Agape love believes the best about people. Agape love is prepared to work through conflict, to find common ground in spite of differences. Paul tells us in 1 Corinthians 13 that agape love is longsuffering and patient and kind. Agape love is not jealous, does not brag, is not arrogant, does not seek its own and is not provoked. Agape love does not take into account a wrong suffered. Agape love does not rejoice in unrighteousness, but rejoices in the truth. Agape love never fails. Agape love is in it for the long haul, because ultimately, he or she representing this love have eternity in mind, they have souls in mind.

Most people function in different forms and levels of eros love, some move up into fileo love, but very, very few move into unconditional agape love. That's because very few people spend enough time in God's presence to actually become like Him so that they can represent His brand which is His nature and His name.

Are you loving *all* people—your family, friends, church, colleagues at work, the cashier at the store, the maintenance person, the homeless person, the person with a different color of skin, the unborn baby? Do you love them sacrificially and unconditionally from God's heart (his value system), or are you actually manipulating them into a relationship with you in order to serve your own interests? Your answer to that question will determine the type of relationships you're in and the type of unity you are building.

Will true Agape love please stand up!

"The Lord descended in the cloud and stood there with him [Moses] as he called upon the name of the Lord. Then the Lord passes by in front of him and proclaimed, 'The Lord, the Lord God, compassionate and gracious, slow to anger, and abounding in lovingkindness and truth; who keeps lovingkindness for thousands, who forgives iniquity, transgression and sin; yet He will by no means leave the guilty unpunished, visiting the iniquity of fathers on the children and on the grand children to the third and fourth generations.' Moses made haste to bow low toward the earth and worship. He said, 'If now I have found favor in Your sight, O Lord, I pray, let the Lord go along in our midst, even though the people are so obstinate, and pardon our iniquity and our sin, and take us as Your own possession.'" – Exodus 34:5-9

It had sleeted all night long, and the outside was a white blanket of ice. This is always a problematic scenario for my silky terrier. In case you didn't know, bathroom duty and snow and ice just don't go together. The moment he set foot on the ice, I knew this was going to be a struggle. My little silky terrier can't handle change. Any change stresses him out, and the first thing that happens when he's anxious is that he won't go to the bathroom. For some reason, he forgets how the plumbing works when he's anxious. Most of us are just the opposite. When our bodies go into adrenaline mode, our bladders do too. Not my little dog!

Here we are in the middle of a winter wonderland, and it's obvious he needs to go, but there's ice on the ground instead of grass. The familiar smells and textures are gone . . . they've been replaced with this cold, slick white stuff, and you know a dog can't relieve himself just anywhere. He looked at me as if to say, "Come on . . . what happened to my favorite bathroom spots? Where did they go?" The fact that he's standing on top of one of his favorite spots makes no difference whatsoever. It's white and icy instead of smelly and grassy green, so he just stands there looking at me with those pitiful eyes, pleading, "Please don't make me do this. Please, I just can't do it."

Meanwhile, I'm coaxing, "Oh, yes, you can. We are not going back into that house until you go, even if we both get frostbite. You're gonna go!" Thirty minutes later, I literally shove an obstinate, shivering dog into the house, with frostbite aggravation I might add, but without success.

In frustration, I think, "God, what is wrong with this dog?" And I hear in my spirit, "Stiff-necked people." My immediate response is, "What do you mean, 'stiff-necked people'? What's that got to do with the dog?" Then it dawned on me. It's got nothing to do with the dog. I had started working on Exodus 33 and 34 for a sermon, and I was wondering where to start, asking God what angle I should approach it from. The answer was, "Stiff-necked people." I was quick to ask, "Did we really have to go through all of that for the answer? Very funny, Lord!"

God says to Moses, *"Go up to a land flowing with milk and honey; for I will not go up in your midst, because you are an obstinate people, because you are a stiff necked people and I might destroy you on the way"* (Exodus 33:3). *Destroy* might be better translated *consume.* Back to the dog . . . while shoving my stiff-necked dog into the house after several unsuccessful trips outside, I was so aggravated that I was about to consume him. "Point well taken, Lord!" Exodus 33:3 says, *"I will not go up in your midst, because you are a stiff necked people lest I consume you along the way."* The God of the Covenant is holy;

and holy and sinful disobedience don't mix. Sin is not able to stand in the presence of holiness. Think of holy as a bonfire and sin as wood. When you throw wood into a fire, the fire automatically consumes it. Fire doesn't have to first think, "Hmm, do I feel like burning wood today or not?" No! You put wood in the fire, and it'll burn. Likewise, sin is combustible in the presence of a fiery, holy Father God. Aren't you glad Jesus came to make us fireproof? So, Father God says to Moses that He'd rather not stay in their midst because if they came too close to Him in their sinful stiff-necked state, they would be consumed. He was thinking about their welfare?

Moses however convinces Father God to accompany them after all, and we know from the rest of the story that some were actually literally consumed by fire, others were swallowed up by the ground, others were bitten by venomous snakes and died, even more died of a plague sent by God, and an entire generation eventually perished in the wilderness, including Moses.

In case you haven't noticed yet, it's risky to invite the Holy of Holies into your life. It'll cost you more than you can imagine. But, and this is the kicker, from a New Testament perspective, Jesus becomes your shield as you move deeper and deeper into the fire of our Holy Father's presence. And unlike wood that burns to ashes, unlike a stiff-necked people that perished, you become pure gold through Jesus while your sin is burned away in the crucible of Father God's fiery presence. The result of that journey of holiness is pure gold demonstrated in selfless agape love.

I'm going to attempt to take you to a place inside Father God where few of His children go, because they fear His holy, fiery presence. They fear the cost of purification. They fear the process of holiness. My prayer is that after today, if you have been held back by that fear, that you will go running into His holy presence, into the Holy of Holies, into that place where His glory resides. I want to take you inside His glory cloud on the mountain. And if you already know that place, I invite you to come along too; hopefully we will explore together new dimensions in that realm of holiness where even you have never been. May God give us each a new revelation of His glory.

Holy friendship with our holy Father inside the glory cloud

"Whenever Moses entered the tent, the pillar of cloud would descend and stand at the entrance of the tent; and the Lord would speak with Moses. When all the people saw the pillar of cloud standing at the entrance of the tent, all the people would arise and worship, each at the entrance of his tent. Thus the Lord used to speak to Moses face to face, just as a man speaks to his friend." – Exodus 33:9-11

If you could choose, do you want to be that person worshiping God from a distance, watching the glory cloud descend on another but never personally entering the cloud and meeting God Himself face to face, or would you want to be Moses who enters in and gets to engage in a true intimate friendship with the holy, living God? The Lord Himself tells us in Numbers 12:8 that He (God) spoke audibly to Moses mouth to mouth in plain audible language, and Moses actually saw a visible form of God. We read further in Deuteronomy 34:10 that Moses knew God face to face, meaning, he knew Him intimately. So, who would you want to be?

Are you the one worshiping from a distance, or are you the one who actually enters into the glory cloud and literally communes with Father God face to face? Both are worshiping, both are honoring God, but only one gets to see Father God's form and hear His audible voice and have true one-on-one communication with Him. Only one gets the kind of revelation and anointing that changes the world around them. Who would you like to be?

Jesus invites us to this kind of inside-the-cloud, intimate friendship in John 15:15 when He says, *"I have called you friends, for all things that I have heard from My Father I have made known to you."* Jesus said, in essence, "I have called you friends and personally shared my Father's heart and mind with you." He was saying to His disciples, "I've taken you into the cloud."

Dear one, do you want to be a worshipful spectator or do you want to be a friend of Jesus, which ultimately leads to intimacy with Father God through Holy Spirit, which ultimately leads to a life of transformation, bringing His Kingdom to earth as it is in heaven? From a New Testament perspective, both are saved, but only one gets to hear the innermost exchange between Holy Father and Son: *"All things that I have heard from My Father I have made known to you."* As a matter of fact, in John 14:23, Jesus discloses that the entire Trinity—Father, Son and Holy Spirit—will actually make their abode in that one who enters into holy friendship with Jesus, that one who enters into the cloud.

A New Testament glory cloud is waiting to descend on a receptive people who will bring the Trinity into our midst like we've never experienced before. The cross and our salvation is only the beginning of our journey into this great, holy, awesome Covenant God we call Father. Most Christians stay at the cross, some venture a little further into Holy Spirit, but few . . . very few . . . allow Jesus and Holy Spirit to take them into the very core, into the very heart and crucible of Father God. That's where pure gold is made; that is where heart transformers are born. But most fear the fiery process required to become pure gold, and so they forfeit the opportunity to meet Father God, just like the Israelites in the wilderness. And in the process, they forfeit the most precious thing anybody can have, which is holy friendship with Holy Father.

When the people of Israel realized that God did not want to accompany them further on their journey, they were devastated. Exodus 33:4 states that they went into mourning. "Oh, no! We are losing God. What are we going to do?" They stripped themselves of all their ornaments and pleasures and sobbed. That is as far as their remorse went though. One man, however, risked everything and in his state of mourning dared to respectfully and boldly approach and confront the living God. Like a Jacob wrestling with God and refusing to let go until God blessed him, Moses went where few people go. It's called holy intercession. It's called risking everything to gain God.

During this holy intercession, he requested the kind of intimacy with God that Jesus later called friendship in John 15:15. It's the kind of intimacy that finds John the disciple leaning on the breast of Jesus, literally snuggling with God, at the dinner table during the last supper. A grown man is snuggling with God who later, on the island of Patmos, comes face to face with the risen Lord, immersed in His glory. This man knew God like very few others do.

Moses risked everything in holy intercession in order to gain God. He prayed, *"Let me know your ways that I may know You, so that I might find favor in Your sight"* (Exodus 33:13). "Lord, I don't want You to leave. Please, teach me how to behave in a way that will cause You to stay. I want to be pleasing to You, Lord. I want You to want me, and I want You to favor me, so show me what pleases You, show me Your ways so that I can learn how to win Your trust and ultimately Your favor—not in a manipulative way, but in an intimate, loving way. Lord, I'm upset at the thought of losing You. I want to spend time with You. I want to know You!"

God's heart is obviously moved, because He responds favorably in verse 14: "Okay, Moses, My presence will go with you and I will give you rest. You want to know My ways. I'll come and live with you and do life with you so that you can get to know Me and my ways. In the process, I will even throw in a bonus called *rest.*" God always gives more than we ask for when we ask with hungry, pure hearts. Holy intercession and the process of being made holy is worth the risk. The reward is God's presence, favor and rest.

Jesus says in Matthew 11:27 and 28, *"Nor does anyone know the Father except the Son, and anyone to whom the Son wills to reveal Him. Come to Me, all who are weary and heavy-laden and I will give you rest."* Moses had the blessing of getting a foretaste of New Testament privilege, but he had to negotiate for it. Jesus has made it available for anybody today who comes to Him. Let me paraphrase the invitation: "Come to Me [Jesus] and I will teach you the ways of our Father and as you learn I personally will take you into our Father's presence where there is favor and rest." Wow, what more could we ask? Presence, favor, and rest! Imagine making these a reality in society! You'd think Moses would stop there, but Moses was on a holy roll.

He boldly asks the Lord for more. In Exodus 33:12-18, Moses cranks it up: "Lord, You say You know me by name. You say I have Your favor. Then show me Your glory. Make Yourself as vulnerable and true before me as I am before You. Uncloak yourself." We read in Numbers that Moses saw

Father God's form; now he wants to see it all. "Uncloak yourself, Father God, so I can know You as intimately as you know me." This is risky stuff!

God's uncloaked, fiery holiness demands nothing but pure gold—everything else will burn. Moses has tasted God and has become so hungry for more that he's willing to risk it all, because he's come to realize the reward is Father God Himself. The reward is uncloaked, intimate, holy friendship with our Father. "Lord, show me Your glory." I imagine all of heaven holding its breath right about that moment. A mortal man immersed in sin, but hungry for God, challenging that same God to uncloak Himself.

This is holiness taking on a whole different dimension. It's where Holiness Himself acknowledges the hunger in a mortal man and says, "Okay, I'll uncloak Myself so you can see and taste My glory. I do have one condition, though—not because I'm holding back, but because I do need to protect you from My holy consuming fire. You can't see My face uncloaked, because if you looked into My eyes uncloaked, you would be consumed. Your mortality cannot look into the windows of My "soul" and live. I will uncloak as much of Myself as your mortality can stand." And all of heaven exhaled as they waited and watched . . . exactly what was Father God going to uncloak?

God gives Moses instruction and tells him to meet Him on the top of the mountain the next morning, and to make sure that no person or animal followed him. He was to come alone. (God does not uncloak Himself to just anybody.) "Come alone, ready to meet Me in my uncloaked form, and be prepared to take notes. Bring two stone tablets, Moses. Better not to bring your laptop, because My presence might fry the hard drive. Bring an old-fashioned stone note slab. You asked to learn My ways. While you're in My presence, I'm going to teach you, and you're eventually going to teach others. In My presence is revelation." This is the kind of revelation that actually sustainably transforms hearts and communities and societies into beautiful oases of His presence, His favor and His rest.

I can hear this reverberating through Paul years later when he prays in Ephesians 1:17, *"May the God of our Lord Jesus Christ, the Father of glory, give to you a spirit of wisdom and of revelation in the knowledge of Him."*

Moses was pulling New Testament privileges into his life because of his hunger for the Father of glory. Oh, might Jesus give us that same hunger! Lord, make us hungry for the Father of glory. We want to enter in. Jesus has paved the way into the Father's heart for anybody and any community and any nation who comes to Him with a humble and repentant and hungry heart. You don't have to be a Moses or a John anymore to enter into this kind of intimacy with the Father of glory. Jesus will take you into the glory cloud to meet Father God, uncloaked, if you ask Him.

I realize some of you might be thinking, why do I need that? Why does society or why do nations need that? Why can't we just be worshipful spectators on the outside? Why would I want to risk my life as I know it to enter into the fiery, holy glory of Father God?

The truth is, there are a few blessings revealed in that cloud that you won't get anywhere else. I believe the main blessing is God's goodness; all the others flow from that, in a sense. Inside this glory cloud on the mountain, God tells Moses in Exodus 33:19, *"I Myself will make all My goodness pass before you."*

Have you experienced all of God's goodness? Do we really have a revelation of all of God's goodness—*all* of His goodness? Inside that cloud, inside that crucible, inside that uncloaked encounter with Father God is the precious, precious revelation of *all* of His goodness . . . goodness that goes beyond all imagination. Father God has a beautiful, tender, loving heart full of goodness that He guards; He reveals it only to those who enter in. Only the Johns who snuggle up against His breast get to experience that level of goodness of His tender heart; but the amazing thing is, anybody in Christ is invited to experience it. Anybody is invited to come and snuggle against His breast, yet, so few do.

That's why we have children of God acting like orphans, because they've never entered in to snuggle. They've never actually tasted the uncloaked goodness of Father God. Exodus 34:6 describes the nature of God's goodness as compassionate, gracious, slow to anger, abounding in lovingkindness and truth to thousands, forgiving iniquity and transgression and sin and even limiting His punishment of the wicked to their third and maybe fourth generation, whereas His lovingkindness goes into the thousandth generation of those who love Him.

Do you need an uncloaked revelation of God's goodness? How would that revelation change your life? How would that revelation change the world? Romans 8:28 tells us, *"And we know that in all things God works for the good of those who love him."* In all things, not just the good things, *all* things, God works for our good. That revelation can come home to roost in your heart, dear one, only when you actually make the effort to leave your tent and take the time to enter into His glory cloud so that you can behold Father God's goodness uncloaked . . . when you take the time to go up the mountain and meet Father God Himself.

This isn't just any kind of goodness. This is pure, unadulterated goodness. It's the kind that takes your breath away and leaves you speechless. It's the fire that burns you until you become pure gold, until you become goodness itself. Everything that is not gold burns, and all that remains is goodness. It's so impactful that it demands holy silence, even to those standing on the outside of the cloud, the spectators. Habakkuk understood this when he said in Habakkuk 2:20, *"The Lord is in His holy temple. Let all the earth be silent before Him."* Zechariah understood this too in Zechariah 2:13 when he said, *"Be silent, all flesh, before the Lord; for He is aroused from His holy habitation."* Even on the outside, the cloud itself demands holy, reverent silence.

But it's even more impactful for the one inside. In Revelation 1, John says he was in the spirit on the Lord's day when Jesus appeared to him in His full glory. John relates that when he saw Him in His glory, he fell at His feet like a dead man. Holy, reverent silence! It's the posture beyond praise, beyond worship. *"Be still and know that I am God."* It's the place of fearful awe and perfect rest. It's where you get to cuddle on His breast in awe and silence, wrapped in His goodness. It's a state of being that, once you've tasted it, you'll never be the same again.

It's the most wonderful, humbling experience you could ever have, and you get to revisit it over and over and over whenever you want. Scripture tells us Moses was the humblest person that ever lived. I believe one of the reasons is that he encountered Father God in His unadulterated, uncloaked goodness. As he burned in that crucible of holy intimacy, he himself was being transformed into goodness itself.

We think God's anger and wrath is impactful, and it is; but it's not anywhere near as impactful as His uncloaked goodness. His goodness is so impactful that the nations of the earth when they "*hear all the good that I [God] do to them; they shall fear and tremble for all the goodness and all the prosperity that I provide for it*" (Jeremiah 33:9). Imagine a goodness that makes you fear and tremble. Imagine demonstrating this goodness of God in your influence circle in such a way that everybody, even those opposing you, is left fearful and trembling, reduced to silence and awe.

A God generation is rising up out of the crucible of Father Gods' presence who are drenched in His agape love. They will engage in warfare against the enemy with a powerful transformational revelation of the goodness of the great I AM! United under God, they will bring salvation and restoration and reformation and transformation to whole communities and nations. Oh, might we be that generation that is brought to fearful awe and reverence and speechlessness because of God revealing His goodness to us. Might we fall like dead men and women at His feet because we beheld His glory, His goodness. That's where true, lasting transformation of the inner man takes place, and it's from there that true, lasting cultural transformation happens.

Are you praying for revival and restoration and reformation that brings Godly transformation not only to the church but to society in general and to nations as a whole? Are you praying for a world where prejudice and divisiveness and self centeredness is trumped by agape love? Ask God to show you His glory, to uncloak His goodness and transform you into goodness yourself. Instead of watching worshipfully as a select few enter in, let's all as one body of Christ enter in, in unison . . . shall we?

"But now faith, hope, love, abide these three; but the greatest of these is love." – 1 Corinthians 13:13

My Father's Arms

Heaven's fields reverberate with life and joy and His Presence,
Laughter echoes on the wings of His wind softly blowing,
Little creatures scamper and play and field grass sway.
Then, music escorts me to a secret place and there He is . . .
Gently smiling, arms stretched out . . . and I run . . .

ABOUT THE AUTHOR

Marlene Ferreira was worshipping in church one morning as a teenager, when all of a sudden the atmosphere changed. Nobody else felt it, only she; it was personal. Holy Spirit came upon her and, all of a sudden, the pulpit shone with the glory of the Lord and she felt a kinship with that pulpit. Her heart started racing and in that moment she knew she would be standing on a Dutch Reformed pulpit preaching as a Dutch Reformed Pastor. Holy Spirit gave her a glimpse of a small part of her future.

In the natural, this was ludicrous. At the time, women were not allowed to pastor Dutch Reformed Churches. Women weren't even allowed to be elders or deacons at that point, let alone pastors. By the grace of God, she received it with faith. She didn't know how God was going to do it, but she believed Holy Spirit.

She achieved a BA degree in Theology and a BTh advanced degree in Theology between 1985 and 1993 at the University of the Free State in South Africa. She also attended a Dutch Reformed Seminary at that same University during that time. On December 6th, 1995 she was ordained as the first woman pastor in the Dutch Reformed Church of her province.

After a few emotional years of opposing segregation in the Dutch Reformed Church, she resigned and moved to America. Currently, she is a volunteer staff member at Grace Covenant Church (GCC) in Roanoke, VA, in America. She works full time in the marketplace while also fulfilling her role as Director of Pastoral Care at GCC (gccroanoke.com).

CPSIA information can be obtained
at www.ICGtesting.com
Printed in the USA
BVHW041738120421
604749BV00014B/344